I0446131

MURDER IN THE RUE MARAT

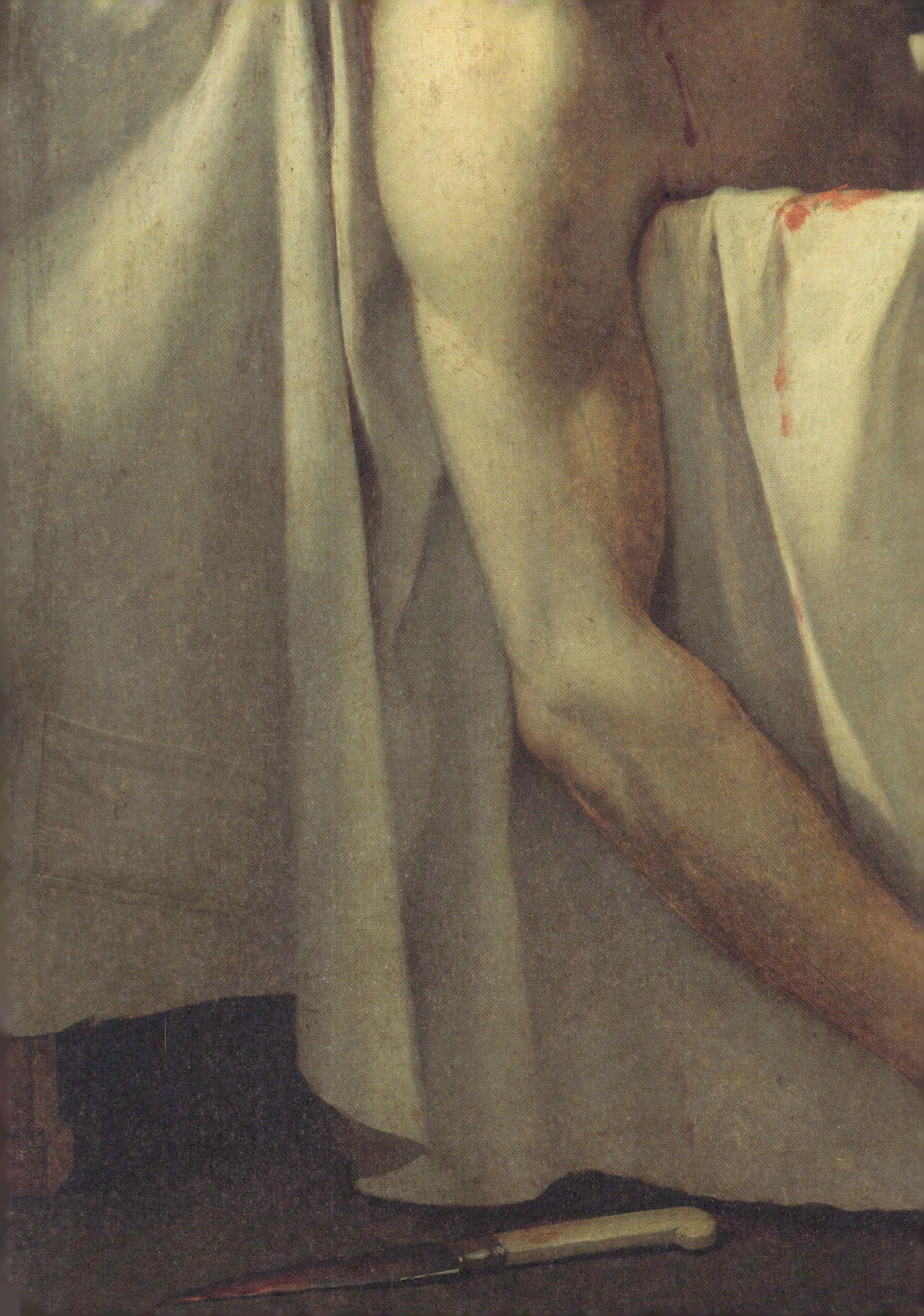

MURDER IN THE RUE MARAT

A Case of Art in Revolution

THOMAS CROW

PRINCETON UNIVERSITY PRESS

Princeton and Oxford

CONTENTS

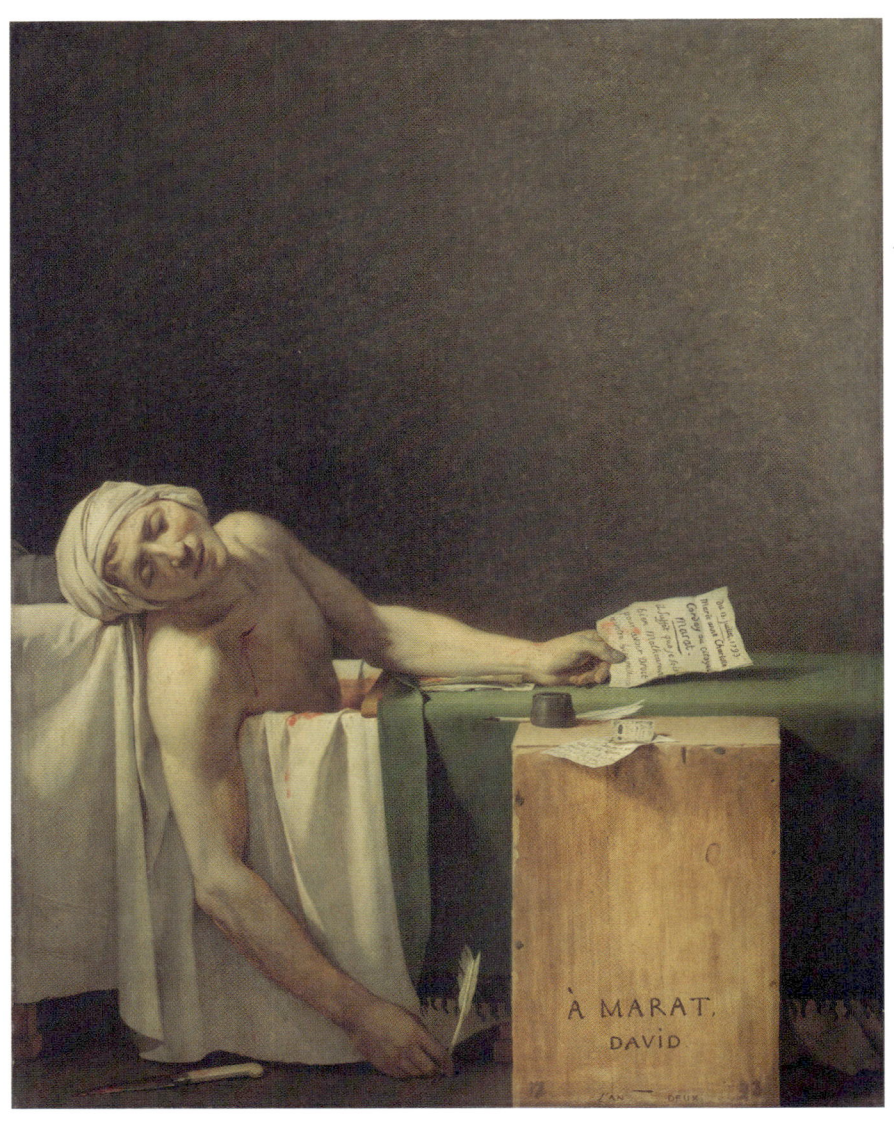

Jacques-Louis David, *Marat at His Last Breath*, 1793, oil on canvas, 165 × 182 cm,
Brussels, Musées royaux d'Art et d'Histoire

I

SCENE-SETTING PROLOGUE

THIS BOOK TAKES ITS WRITER back to a beginning, back to an unrealized moment in my first grappling with art, history, and what passed in the day for the theory of both. In the service of that undertaking, I break with the habit of a lifetime in no longer avoiding the first-person voice. But the core subject here is not my life experience, but one of the best-known, most memorable, and widely reproduced paintings in the western canon, *The Death of Marat* being only one of its competing titles; another being *Marat Assassinated* and a third, the dramatic *Marat at His Last Breath* [*facing page*]; its author, the radical French Revolutionary Jacques-Louis David; its fashioning in the early autumn of 1793, part and parcel of a political watershed leading to what is known as the Great Terror. This present endeavor to understand David's work in as many of its dimensions as possible begins, nonetheless, by circling back to the moment the *Marat* seized my youthful imagination so compellingly that I planned to devote my prospective years of doctoral research to this one object alone. How and why did this eccentric plan come to me? Why did it not happen? And why revive it now?

It would seem unremarkable to note that David's *Death of Marat* first came to me via a reproduction. That would be the case with most works of art for most people. But this reproduction was far from a normal, photographically printed illustration; it was a hand-rendered copy by Robert Wilson, the accomplished monumental sculptor, part-time rock-poster artist, and nurturer of two orphan tapirs from infancy, he and his wife being active in the conservation of the species. A crisply drawn tapir profile sometimes served for his signature, as did a similar profile rendering of a bison. The latter emblem graces one corner of his poster for an appearance by the San Francisco band Moby Grape in September 1968 at a club in the oceanside Los Angeles suburb of Torrance, the main motif of the poster being a freehand, heavily modeled rendering of David's *Death of Marat* [*facing page*]. Any connection between David's martyr portrait and the accomplished but somewhat generic music of the advertised band is elusive. Indeed, when Wilson came to craft a flyer for a later concert in Claremont by no less an artist than the blues master Muddy Waters, a musician of incomparable stature and gravity, he re-used the same drawing, where the juxtaposition seems to make a great deal more sense. Nothing could have kept me away from the concert, and I carry an indelible impression of the deep-red stock on which Wilson's repurposed Marat was printed, despite never having seen it since (as Wilson's legacy is sadly vanishing).

As best as I can reconstruct, my first imagined project to secure professional credentials as an art historian ultimately rested on the memory of that revelatory moment. One could well ask how this secondary rendering could compare with even a standard reproduction of the magisterial original canvas. Little in evidence is the immense dignity and composure of the original, David's inspired synthesis of monumental funerary portraiture with an interlocked constellation of accessory objects that conjure the offstage assassin, Charlotte Corday. Nor is there much to be seen of the severely rectilinear compositional scheme and the broodingly undefined background that occupies half the canvas. Wilson's vignette dispenses with virtually all of this. Likewise, nowhere in evidence are the samples of writing meant to signal both the saintly benevolence of the martyr and

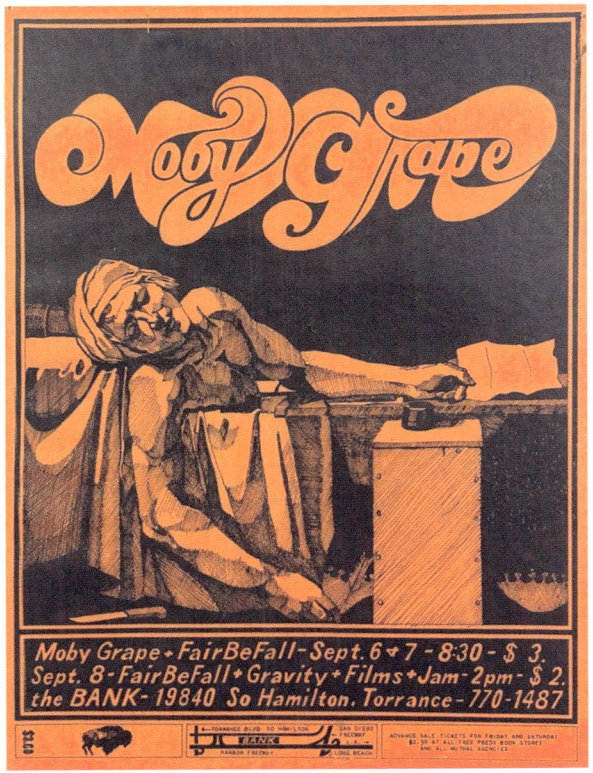

Robert Wilson, offset print poster (Moby Grape
at the Bank, Torrance, Calif.), 1969, 22 × 28 cm

the plot points of his demise. One can barely find the fatal wound.
The roughly fashioned crate on which Marat writes—an economical tour-de-force of David's naturalistic technique—is narrowed
and divested of detail. Only the inkpot remains among the telling
instruments of the subject's muck-raking journalistic vocation. But
perhaps Wilson offers something else by way of compensation, most

notably in the shape of the body transformed into a buckled relief of emphatic planes of an almost cubist character. Both his omissions and his distortions arguably suit the demands of line work meant to stand out on a cheap, offset handbill.

In my account of persistent memory, Wilson's poster motif manages to look like memory, with all the lacunae and exaggerations that characterize testimony from recollection—unintentionally in keeping with the forensic character of his model. If I am finding a point of origin for my own Marat fascination in Wilson's appropriation, the question naturally arises how might the idea have come to him? There is no way to know for certain, but an overwhelmingly likely prompt had arrived in the previous year with the release in 1967 of Peter Brook's film of his own London theater production *The Persecution and Assassination of Jean-Paul Marat as Performed by the Inmates of the Asylum of Charenton under the Direction of the Marquis de Sade*. Written and first staged in 1964 by the German author Peter Weiss, Brook's production for the Royal Shakespeare Company had opened the following year, in a translation by Geoffrey Skelton along with the compelling addition of songs by Adrian Mitchell and Richard Peaslee in the tradition of Kurt Weill's collaborations with Bertolt Brecht. A long Broadway run followed, while the popular folk singer Judy Collins opened one side of her 1966 album *In My Life* with a medley from the play—her title song linking the Beatles to Mitchell's vaudeville-like chants, in which the name Marat is repeated over and over. How many among its half-million buyers asked themselves, who was this person?

Weiss had found his pretext in two points of historical data that by themselves entail extremes of social emancipation, violence, sexual excess, and coercion of vulnerable bodies: first, the perennially incarcerated marquis de Sade, during a rare spell of liberty under the Revolution, had delivered a memorial eulogy for the murdered Marat at a meeting of his neighborhood assembly or section; and second,

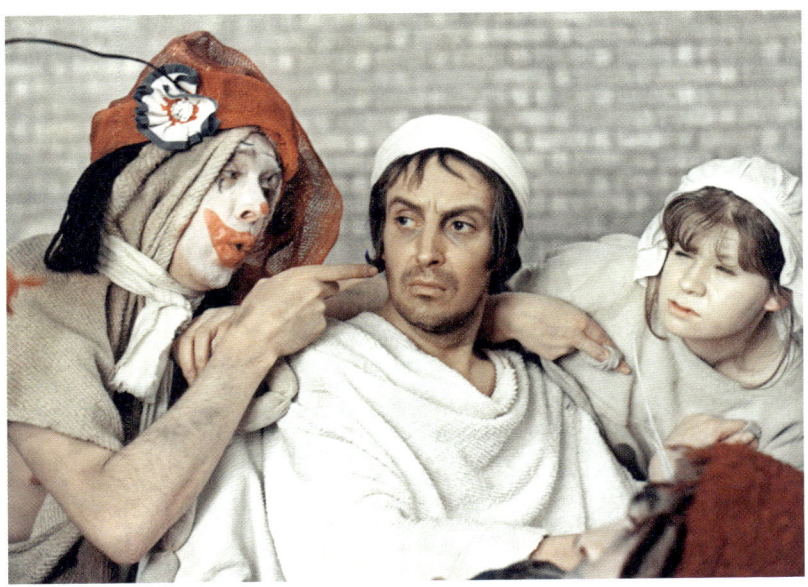

Scene from Peter Weiss's *The Persecution and Assassination of Jean-Paul Marat as Performed by the Inmates of the Asylum of Charenton under the Direction of the Marquis de Sade*, dir. Peter Brook, Old Vic, London, 1965

Sade was transferred in 1803 from prison to the asylum at Charenton on the eastern edge of Paris, where he remained until his death in 1814. During that time, the hospital director, enlightened for his time, believed in the rehabilitative potential of art and thus encouraged Sade's literary pursuits. Among these were plays performed by his fellow inmates under his direction. On these bare bones, Weiss embroidered an imaginary performance devoted to Marat's assassination, a play within a play, each of the main characters exhibiting a distinct mental disorder [*above*]. Corday, for example, suffers from narcolepsy, needing to be woken when she has a line to deliver or an action to perform, while the paranoiac playing

Marat varies least from the historical actuality of his character. In the play's German title, Weiss specifies, "performed by the acting company [*die Schauspielgruppe*] of the asylum," which implies the analogy with the experimental troupes of his time.

As is also known, well-off Parisians were invited to witness these productions as a form of philanthropic if voyeuristic entertainment. Weiss supplies such an audience in the family of the asylum director, smug at the start only to be overwhelmed in panic at the end, as the inmates, aroused by Sade's exhortations to "Revolution . . . Copulation," break though the proscenium and must be suppressed by the attendants in a violent melee. Weiss's play has entered the repertoire and continues to be regularly performed all over the world, but these scattered revivals can no more than suggest the extraordinary force carried in the general culture by Brook's staging, as it became a major event in the contemporaneous unfolding of the counterculture. "Marat/Sade" brought to generational consciousness earlier cognate experiments in immersive theater carried on by the Polish visionary Jerzy Grotowski or the Living Theater of Judith Malina and Julian Beck, who had been effectively exiled by hostile authorities from New York to Europe in the early 1960s for trafficking in outlawed subject matter. According to the veteran London theater critic Michael Coveney, Brook's staging not only "launched the fringe and alternative theatre in this country, representing an intersection between European theory and new British radicalism," but it "changed the lives of most people who saw it."[1]

That moment may seem elusive now; indeed, many culturally aware people have no recollection of "Marat/Sade" at all, despite the weighty symbolic salience of its early incarnations. The film, a literal document of the stage play filmed in seventeen days, makes plain that David's mise-en-scène guided the visual presentation of the climactic event [*facing page*]. It is, indeed, difficult to imagine Weiss fleshing out his scenario without having the painting in mind.

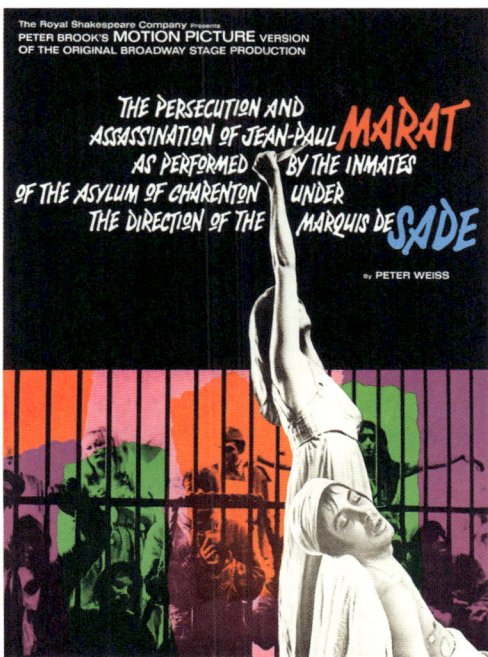

Publicity poster for the film, *The Persecution and
Assassination of Jean-Paul Marat as Performed by
the Inmates of the Asylum of Charenton under the
Direction of the Marquis de Sade*, from the play by
Peter Weiss, dir. Peter Brook, United Artists, 1967

The marquis de Sade obviously required no introduction to modern
audiences, but the physically unprepossessing Marat, known to history more as a hidden fugitive than as a public actor, survives above
all through David's representation.

My inward memory-retrieval of David's painting thus entailed
retrieving from partial amnesia at least one monument that defined
the countercultural 1960s for those living through it, that excavation

unearthing the political contestation, incendiary violence, cultivated madness, and radical egalitarianism that found expression in this emblem of long-past political martyrdom. The uncanny character of "Marat/Sade" lies in its having come in advance of the counter-cultural flowering it came so closely to mirror. Its composition, beginning well before its German premiere in 1964, preceded the manifestations of these dissident phenomena from 1965 onward. Weiss revised the play more than once in its early years, a process in which Brook and his collaborators then assumed an active role.

Other contemporaneous developments jibed with it in almost uncanny ways. Between the London opening and its capture on film, the celebrity anti-psychiatrist R. D. Laing joined in founding an uncompromisingly egalitarian, therapeutic community in the city's East End. The renegade Scottish therapist had found fame with a series of studies arguing that the schizophrenic exhibits sane coping mechanisms in the face of unmanageable family dynamics—that is, opts out of oppressive societal norms in microcosm. Just as the overseer of the stage-asylum at Charenton (mischaracterized by Weiss as a bourgeois prig) faces his charges rising up with demands for equality ("We're all normal and we want our freedom!"), Laing and his professional colleagues were doing their best to live communally among their disturbed patients without distinction of rank or role. Weiss's alliance of the lucid Sade with his impaired colleagues had already been modeling such a therapeutic pact.

Period demands for equality arising from the American civil rights movement had thus widened to include emancipation of the furthest class of disenfranchised outcasts. An echo sounds of Michel Foucault's thesis "Folie et Déraison: Histoire de la folie à l'âge classique," written at the end of the 1950s (but only belatedly published in English as the abridged *Madness and Civilization*), his being the foundational argument of the era that mental illnesses were constructed socially as exemplary forms of medicalized exclusion, effected in the service of normative obedience and social control. In an intriguing convergence, Foucault had written his treatise during a period of teaching and study in Stockholm, where Peter Weiss also lived and worked. Laing, for his part, duly laid claim in 1966 to the then-obscure French thinker as a precursor, just as he also embraced the American acid guru Timothy Leary and the therapeutic uses of LSD (with much personal experimentation). The two together conjoined involuntary derangement with purposeful mind expansion as linked paths to overthrowing policed cognitive conformity.

Long after this peak moment of cultural salience, "Marat/Sade" maintains its uncanny ability to anticipate events, as does its touchstone in David's martyr-portrait. Even the arch-historicizer Otto Karl Werckmeister (one of my graduate teachers) lambasted the folly of explicating the painting only in the frame of its own moment, as if there were nothing left in the *Marat* for anyone to discover and put to use after 1793. From those new uses emerge revelations of overlooked meaning invested there from the start. He illustrates the point with a revival of Weiss's play in 2000: "The Berliner Ensemble, Bertolt Brecht's old company," he writes, "extolled Marat's revolutionary tenacity as a paragon of resistance against the social injustice brought by East Germany's ruthless conversion to a capitalist economy. As the curtain rose, the stage still dark, the asylum inmates performed a whispered, cacophonous recital of Gertrud Kolmar's defiant paean *To Marat,* written in 1933 as a secret protest against Hitler's rise to power. The Jewish poet would live through ten years of Nazi oppression until her murder at Auschwitz sometime in the early spring of 1943."[2]

•

Such were the forces of cultural and political change piled up behind the apparition of Marat on Robert Wilson's poster in the autumn of 1968. Storing it away in the back of my mind, I would not yet have collated my exposure to the screen version of "Marat/ Sade" alongside Laing's *Divided Self* or Leary's *Psychedelic Experience* —throw in Ken Kesey's *One Flew over the Cuckoo's Nest* and Gregory Bateson's *Steps to an Ecology of Mind*. But I did carry with me some recent memories that resonated with the revolutionary rants voiced by the *enragé* character of Jacques Roux in Weiss's script. A previous semester spent in France had culminated with my Pomona College companions and I arriving in Paris on 1 May 1968, settling into Latin Quarter digs, and then marveling as all hell promptly erupted around us. Unknowingly, we had chosen a small hotel that lay in the old Cordeliers district, where Marat had sheltered among such Jacobin luminaries as Georges Danton and Camille Desmoulins (the former rue des Cordeliers became la rue Marat in 1793–94, the source of this book's Poe-indebted title). Just to lean out of the window of my hotel was to see student insurgents waving red and black flags from the roof of the imposing Odéon theater at the top of the street. On 10 May, witnessing the enormous barricade being erected at the angle formed by the rues Saint-Jacques and Gay-Lussac— whole automobiles stacked within an improvised edifice of paving stones, traffic signs, stanchions, grates, and liberated construction debris—in an atmosphere of jubilant shouts and chants, lycéens joining their older brothers and sisters, small fires glowing as night fell, it all seemed to make vivid and actual all the famous street rebellions stretching back to 1789. We had left before the tear-gassing, head-cracking CRS (state security police) goons moved in during the early hours of the morning [*facing page*]. A few inconsequential bruises came later, since it was impossible for a young person to walk in that neighborhood without a roving patrol at some point teaching you a lesson.

No such excitement, obviously, lay in the far eastern suburbs of Los Angeles on our return. But it was a heady time, nonetheless, for art in the small college town of Claremont. Figures of enduring

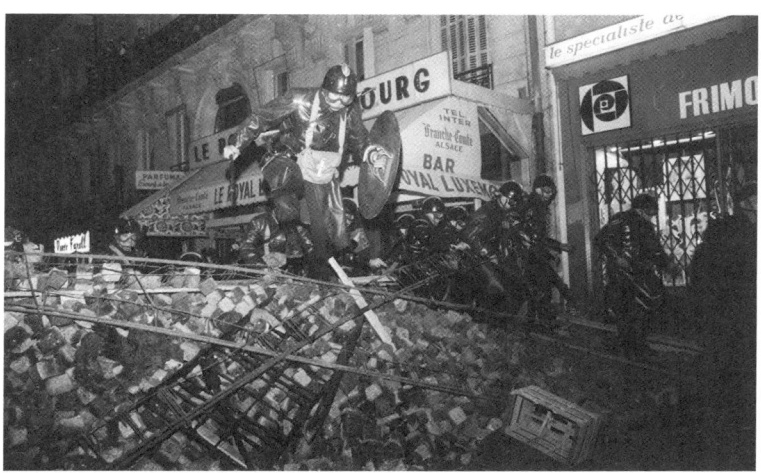

Gökşin Sipahioğlu, 10 May 68, rue Gay-Lussac, Paris CRS riot policeman wielding
shields and batons cross a barricade to charge striking students near
the Sorbonne, SIPA Press

importance in art history, among them our Pomona contemporary
Chris Burden, alongside light conjurer Jim Turrell, worldly expat-
riate Bas Jan Ader, droll but razor-sharp Al Ruppersberg, austerely
aloof Lewis "Duke" Baltz, opaquely intense Jack Goldstein, absorbed
student of the senses Michael Asher, and self-abnegating, Kyoto-
born Hiro Kosaka, were all present (my loss that artists of commensurable stature formed at Pomona, like Helen Pashgian, Barbara
T. Smith, and Judy Fiskin, had by then migrated to other parts of
California). As I look back, their work constitutes some of the
strongest art being made anywhere at the time, which I've argued
elsewhere more than once. Even lacking that art-historical perspective at the time, all I knew was that I did not want to leave that world,
which had made me care about art in the first place.[3]

•

At first, I briefly took up studio training by talking my way into the Master of Fine Arts program at the Claremont Graduate School, where Robert Wilson had matriculated and both Turrell and Baltz were then simultaneously MFA students and teachers. Having failed, however, to find in myself the consuming vocation that makes a good artist as opposed to a merely passable one, I fell back for the moment on a certain knack for the psychedelic graphic idiom, though in a manner shamefully imitative of Wilson (just as my paintings were abjectly derivative of Ed Ruscha). To a lesser degree, I was channeling from a distance the reigning master of cross-hatched technique and my real artistic idol, Rick Griffin, once a high-school surfing cartoonist from Palos Verdes, by then grown into an artist with magisterial command of the baroque poster idiom for the Grateful Dead and the ballrooms of hippie San Francisco. I borrowed from both fine cross-hatching, using temperamental Rapidograph drafting pens, networks of overlayed lines worked around areas of unrelieved black, with lettering incorporated into the hand-drawn composition. One free-lance example [*facing page*] was commissioned by the local artists' bar and hangout in exchange for a $25 tab—a reasonable sum in those days. The image, taken from a photograph I found in *Rolling Stone*, plays up the Left's ironizing of the American flag that Jasper Johns had begun a decade before, along with, I guess, the mime chic that Antonioni's 1966 film *Blow-Up* had made current. Nor was I above using these techniques elsewhere, if more discreetly, to support myself by imparting a pastoral feeling to the print advertising of a local subdivision developer. When I left that job for graduate school, Wilson's spouse, Sheryl Todd, took my place, which I thought made some restitution on my debt.

Making it to graduate school, however, would not be straight-forward. The choice of art history had been occasioned by my leap into studio art, in that I had been required to make up prerequisites in the subject that I had never acquired. Some excellent instructors in

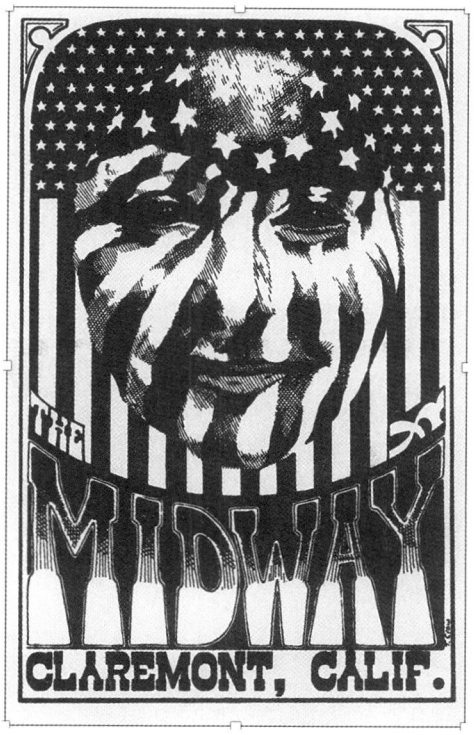

Thomas Crow, silkscreen poster
(Midway Inn), 1970, 29 × 17 cm

Claremont made the discipline seem feasible and attractive. But I would be one of those semi-autodidact applicants dreaded by admissions committees. Yale (where I would one day chair the department) took a pass, and I gave up on the East Coast. No great surprise, in that I had been doing little to fill in my patchy basic knowledge of the field. Instead, prompted by my unorthodox instructor in Native American arts, Karl Hertel, I had turned to the structuralism of

French anthropologist Claude Lévi-Strauss, in over-ambitious expectations of gaining powers of synthetic understanding beyond textbook points of information. I was almost certainly working out my fascination with all things French, but that excursion taught me a lot and remains with me. As this powerful mode of inquiry has lost a great deal of the currency it then enjoyed, a brief sketch might be in order of what I found so compelling in his grand project, where else it led, and how David's *Marat* reappeared at the end of it.

•

Lévi-Strauss had begun by analyzing kinship patterns in traditional societies, which demonstrated that apparent absence of technological complexity finds compensation in extraordinary systems of internalized social rules and environmental knowledge. He followed this foundational project with one of even greater scope, as he sought to map the universe of indigenous mythology across the entire New World with commensurate rigor. At the core of his method was unbundling the densely colorful trappings of linear mythic tales in order to isolate the bare concepts or qualities they embody, then to correlate these terms relationally, irrespective of their ostensible narrative functions. The philosopher Vincent Descombes succinctly summarizes the abstract, binary logic involved:

> The significance of his characters and their adventures is determined in advance by the rules governing the tales of this particular cultural domain. If, for example, oppositions such as "giant/dwarf" or "princess/shepherdess" should be significant within this code, then the size and occupation of the characters are no longer a matter of choice. Consequently the narrator of a myth is simply actualizing the possibilities inherent in the code, or in the signifying system to which he submits in order to speak. In the end, it is indeed the structure that decides what may—sometimes what must—be said on a given occasion.[4]

All the fantastical personages and exploits, couplings and catastrophes function simultaneously to animate and to cloak the parsimonious bundle of abstract traits at the core of any mythological cycle. No compendium of discrete stories, myth exists less in a corpus than in a ramified network of correspondences, filiations, variants, repetitions, and effects at a distance. As Lévi-Strauss elucidates, "The question of significance does not arise at the level of each myth taken in isolation but at that of the system of which they form the elements."[5]

As I still understand it from those days, myths fundamentally exist for their tellers and listeners as a way of handling the irreconcilable paradox at the heart of human existence: the clash between Nature, which bestows biological being, and Culture, which confers social identity. The universal prohibition against incest, which Lévi-Strauss posits as present in some form in every society, serves to impose the logic of the code on raw life. Only by virtue of that stricture can two physically cognate individuals of a given sex come under starkly opposed social signs: this one you may marry; this one you may not. That binary carries the survival benefit of group solidarity and cooperation by mandating the exchange of marriage partners beyond immediate family groups—the individual's initiation into all further systems of symbolic exchange, myth prominent among them, following from that primary submission to binary, signifying logic. The telling of tales cannot reconcile what is irresolvable nor satisfactorily explain away this inescapable fissure in human self-awareness, but can continue to juggle the terms of the paradox, keeping it both in play and at bay.

Such myths may originally be collective, authorless fictions, but, nonetheless, cannot be separated from self-conscious artistic endeavor. The visual and literary arts of the west could barely exist without their substratum of inherited Greco-Roman mythology; indeed, Lévi-Strauss framed his 1955 manifesto essay, "The Structural

Study of Myth," around the foundational Greek Oedipus cycle, before turning to unexpected but persuasive parallels in the origin stories of North American Puebloans. There thus seemed to me an obvious bridge from structuralist anthropology to the study of art, one that no one seemed to be traversing.

While I was immersing myself in these quandaries, I hadn't known that Lévi-Strauss was on the verge of publishing his application of structuralist logic to the realm of sculpture. His remarkable *Way of the Masks* (*La Voie des masques*), published in 1975, parses the transformational logic that had governed exchanges of ritual objects between the Salish and Kwakwaka'wakw groups in what is now southern British Columbia. Even in the case of the smoothly modeled and vividly expressive forms of the latter, he proved abundantly able to subject art to the same conceptual unbundling and systematic reconfiguration as he had the linguistic terminology of myths. But there had already emerged from the Parisian forcing house of theory a work of interpretation that applied similar principles of analysis to one representative aesthetic object, in this case a text it then proceeded to unbundle clause by clause to expose a core logic analogous to Lévi-Strauss's master dichotomy between Nature and Culture.

Published in 1970 under the name of literary scholar and semiotician Roland Barthes and cryptically titled *S/Z*, it constitutes something of a report on the shared work of a Paris seminar led by Barthes over two years in the late 1960s.[6] The exclusive object of the endeavor was an early text by Honoré de Balzac, really little more than a story, published in 1830 under the title *Sarrasine*.[7] Its eponymous protagonist is a young French sculptor dispatched in 1758 from Paris to Rome, where he was expected to refine his craft in the presence of the city's exemplary monuments and masterpieces. But the ostensible masterpiece on which he fixates is a living one: La Zambinella, the reigning diva of the Roman musical stage. The drama turns on the naïve foreign artist's misunderstanding of local custom—there could be no public female performers in the Papal States—thus his misrecognition of the singer's physical identity as a castrated male. Though repeatedly warned away from his pursuit of the singer, the headstrong Sarrasine, deaf to every intimation of the truth, resorts to kidnapping the object of his affection. Enlightenment comes too late to prevent his murder at the hands of henchmen dispatched by the castrato's powerful protector, the sinister Cardinal Cicognara.

Balzac nests that story within another, a framing narrative set in the time of its writing, more particularly amid the decadence of the late Bourbon Restoration as the Revolution of 1830 looms. During an opulent Paris soirée, hosted by a family of mysterious origin and fortune, the narrator attempts to beguile his own love interest with the story behind the spectral presence at the party of an ancient personage of indeterminate gender, adorned in eerily vampiric finery. This apparition proves, of course, to be La Zambinella in old age, the source of the fortune enjoyed by her collateral descendants. Balzac contrives a stark antithesis by having the wizened, bejeweled castrato enter the room in which hangs the painted image of the nude statue modelled by Sarrasine from transports of memory and imagination in the solitude of his studio. Copied once in fiction, its real counterpart (though disguised as a replica after Vien for the purposes of the story) is evoked by the narrator for the benefit of his listener and the reader: Anne-Louis Girodet's *Sleep of Endymion*, depicting the radiantly androgynous young hunter put to sleep in eternal physical perfection by the infatuated moon goddess [*page 18*].

Ample evidence exists that Balzac indeed wove the tale around his fascination with Girodet's 1791 painting, to which he had made great efforts to gain access.[8] And both text and canvas would now be amply open to interpretation under a rubric of non-binary identity and desire. But Barthes's analytical aim, despite his own gay life, led him to emphasize rather than relax the conventional distinction

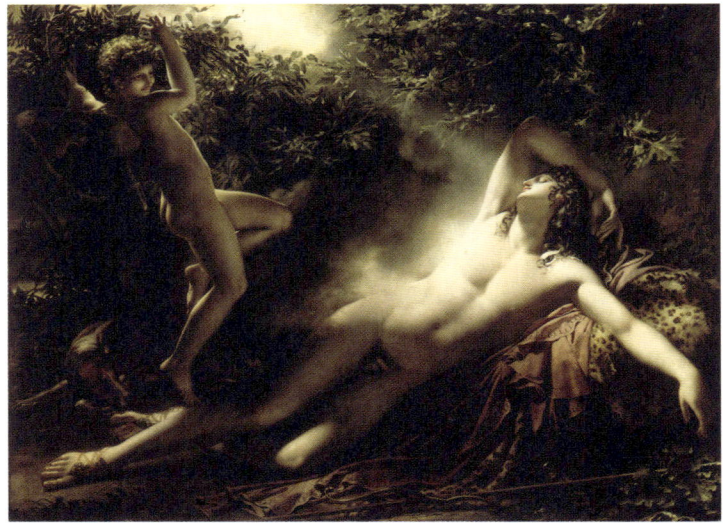

Anne-Louis Girodet, *The Sleep of Endymion*, 1791, oil on canvas,
197 × 261 cm, Paris, Musée du Louvre

between the genders. Following Freud via the *au courant* French analyst Jacques Lacan, successful repression of the terrifying fantasy of castration marks the passage from the plenitude of infantile Nature to a procrustean Culture ruled by threatening fathers. The child's imaginary sexual rivalry with a parent seeds Lévi-Strauss's macro-prohibition against incest into the micro-formation of the individual subject, where entry into the signifying order entails unconscious disavowal of both desire for the mother and terror at the father's castrating revenge (male being the default gender for reasons of chauvinistic convenience). The scandalous anecdote on which the story of Sarrasine turns thus becomes the scandal of representation itself. Once made explicit in the story, the horror of castration brings the exchange of signs to an abrupt end. As Sarrasine falls to the assassins' blades, he excoriates his former love object: "Monster! . . . You have wiped women from the earth";[9] and the woman pursued by the narrator in the fictive present withdraws from him in horror; "Leave me," she commands, their implied sexual contract nullified.

In Barthes's telling, Girodet's *Endymion* can be no more than a weak attempt to assert the impossible wholeness of the body unmarked by the void of castration, and it is accordingly treated with relative indifference as just one iteration in a myth-like chain of replicas. But the granularity of the Barthes seminar's systematic parsing of virtually every detail of a suitably concise object of analysis—each word-cluster assigned a value within one of an interlocking set of codes—struck me with some excitement as approximating the model I was seeking. Even in a short narrative, Barthes's procedure populated a teeming universe of interlocking signs at least analogous in scope to the one encompassing the myths recorded in the annals of anthropology. As such, these particles of narrative become likewise susceptible to unbundling and reconfiguration in some atemporal, tabular array.

In both its macro- and micro-applications, structuralist thought carried the liberating promise of freedom from hidebound humanist ideologies, so seeming to me continuous with the ethos of self-exploration that saturated California culture at the end of the 1960s. But what work of visual art would become my *Sarrasine*? It would be some years down my professional road before I took the obvious bait and profitably followed up Balzac's broad hints about Girodet's *Endymion*, but that wasn't really the one.[10] As broached at the outset of this introduction, it was David's *Death of Marat*, while not obviously related to *S/Z*, that first appeared before me. With the benefit of hindsight, David's crafting of monumental formality out of modest, homely elements must have struck home. The painting possessed a compactness and simplicity on a par with *Sarrasine*, that likeness enhanced by the common core of gendered violence in both, with the sexual positions of the main actors hidden, displaced, or disguised: the portion of Marat's naked body below the rib cage lies out of view, nor is there even the suggestion of a setting beyond the bare items of still life crowded against the foreground plane. As for the fatal wound itself, to adopt Barthes's Freudian register, the very discretion of the nearly bloodless incision makes the fatal injury loom larger, testifying to the unseen, pitiless female assailant widely characterized in her time as a beguiling object of erotic fascination.

But how to unbundle and reconfigure an already atemporal array of signifiers? My hypothetical plan was to reverse Barthes's procedure and find a way to render sequentially the non-linear, atemporal painting. What I imagined was applying what drawing ability I possessed (long before Photoshop) to model portions of the traced composition, so that any given component of the work's internal symbolic dialogue would stand out from the others, the resulting sheets ultimately constituting an interleaved analogue to the spatial redistribution of narrative achieved by Lévi-Strauss and Barthes.

In 2002, the Chinese painter Yue Minjun exhibited a finely painted, identically sized replica of David's *Death of Marat*, with the conspicuous subtraction from the composition of the figure of Marat himself [*facing page*]. This canvas is by no means the first that Yue has adapted from an esteemed French original, but his previous modus operandi has been to populate his prototypes—Delacroix's *Liberty at the Barricades*, for example—with versions of his signature personage, a grinningly cartoonish self-portrait. But he stopped short of this parodic effect in the face of the funereal gravity of the *Marat*, reversing course by attempting no substitution at all. While that decision may have followed from the dynamics of his own oeuvre, the evident force of Yue Minjun's *Death of Marat* lends suggestive concreteness to the concept I had long ago imagined for art history, that the means of interpretation could at least begin in its own non-textual medium.

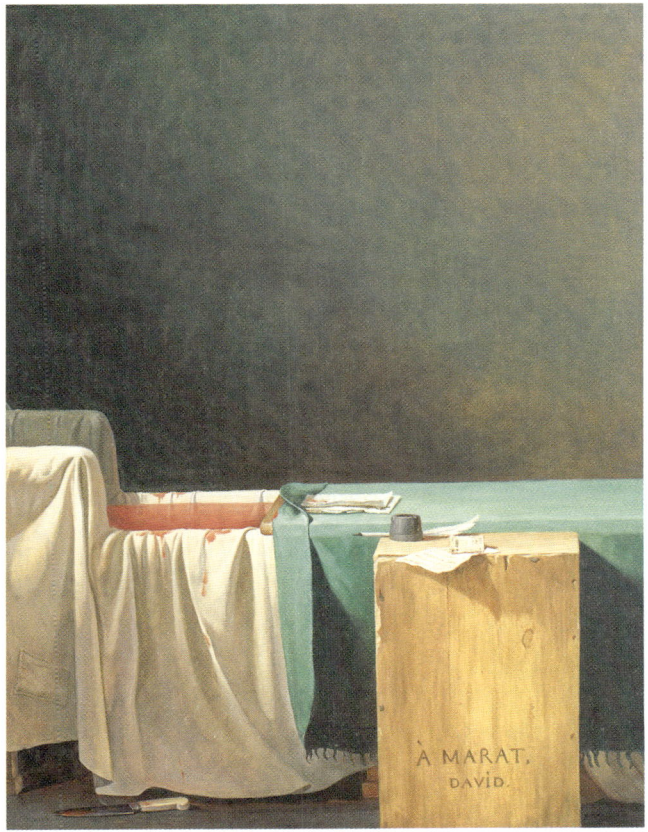

Yue Minjun, *The Death of Marat*, 2002,
oil on canvas, 290 × 219 cm, private collection

But there would need to be more and finer operations on the painting than even so vivid an exercise as this one. It was foundational
for Roland Barthes that the effect of unity impressed on readers by
a well-crafted story, poem, or novel is just that, an effect, whereby

the author has succeeded in suturing into apparent coherence all the disparate, partial precedents mixed into its generic container. That insight applies all the more aptly to works of visual art, as made plain by the preoccupations of old-fashioned art historians with influences, borrowings, and sources. These were generally not wrong, but what should have been intermediate steps toward understanding took the place of its ends. An interpretive vehicle was needed that answered to a higher-order recognition that an apparently singular work is in fact many partial works at once. One way to proceed on the basis of this postulate, it had struck me, would be to transform the painting by varied subtractions, generating a series or gallery of separate works, each to be considered in turn, before letting them collapse at the end back into the whole.

Within the academic profession of art history at this juncture, such a proposal would have been met with incomprehension in virtually any graduate program, if not serious worry about my professional suitability. It proved a stroke of luck that I had simply pursued the local option for graduate study, the University of California, Los Angeles, then a lightly regarded outpost of the discipline far from its vigilant centers in the Northeast (and where I found the fantastic encouragement of peers like Holly Clayson, Leonard Folgarait, Serge Guilbaut, and Mimi Yiengpruksawan, all destined for the upper echelon of the profession). My fascination with ethnography had led me there, my initial mentor being the remarkable, undersung Africanist Arnold Rubin. Having returned from extensive research in the arid Benue Valley of northern Nigeria, Rubin had found himself missing that immersion in the totality of ritual life that lent inert, portable objects their full meanings. His Super-8 films and vivid stories captured the ways in which masks and power objects were presented, manipulated, and worn on ceremonial occasions. The Los Angeles artist Betye Saar, for one, regularly credited his 1975 *Artforum* article, "Accumulation: Power and Display in African Sculpture," as informing her conviction that collage components could work on viewers in an active manner that exceeded static contemplation.[11]

Rubin likewise insisted that ritual abounded in present-day America, ready to be unpacked by eyes attuned to this African attitude toward worked objects as spirit instruments. Looking around the Los Angeles basin for a stimulating substitute, he lighted on the Tournament of Roses parade in Pasadena, a year-around enterprise with forthcoming informants and richly ephemeral aesthetic practices. His seminars on the subject drew his students into participatory forms of learning that militated against the status hierarchies that ruled the discipline. One could make a valid claim that Rubin pioneered the para-discipline of Visual Culture, but too soon to gain traction for the tremendous expansion in available subjects that he had conceived. I feel that the range and curiosity present in all my subsequent work owes as much to his tutelage as to any other influence.

To Rubin's disappointment, my nerve began to fail, in ways that do me no credit, at the prospect of a long sojourn on my own in the African backcountry. That hesitation coincided with the arrival on the UCLA faculty of the young, then-little-known English art historian T. J. Clark, one of the few practitioners who could make western painting sing with the intellectual panache of a Roland Barthes. So my new path was set, or so I thought. Clark knew his way around all of the theoretical models I was attempting to master and seemed encouraging when I brought him the Marat proposal. His immediate advice, sensible to be sure, was that I needed to know a lot more about the French art of the eighteenth century. That catching up, as it turned out, stretched into a couple of decades, which yielded two books, *Painters and Public Life in Eighteenth-Century Paris* and *Emulation: Making Artists for Revolutionary France*, accompanied by a fairly fraught professional odyssey through the aforementioned East

Coast citadels of the discipline. Those professional vicissitudes sent me into writing mainly on modern and contemporary art, where I found friendlier colleagues, while my original project, that thing I wanted to do as a fledgling doctoral candidate, somehow got lost. But recently it began to beckon from the past, like a kind of lost chord, just as structuralism's bygone moment likewise calls out for reconsideration, its worthy legacies deserving rescue from the condescension and amnesia of present-day intellectual fashion.

Both aims have figured in the foregoing self-examination as to how David's *Death of Marat* came so forcefully to my mind in the first place, that excavation having connected with the multiple currents of 1960s dissent that have dominated much of my intervening scholarly work, themes that found unexpected expression in this emblem of long-past political martyrdom. For all of the recondite abstractions entailed in its intellectual points of departure, the aim of this study will be to reconnect the painting with the lives of its creator and his subject. Only two individuals, to be sure, but both could be instanced as exemplars of lives enacted in public for public purposes. Both came marked by highly particularizing physical disfigurement: Marat's livid skin inflammations and David's pronounced tumorous growth on one cheek. But these traits only underwrote their bearers' generalized identities as, respectively, the Friend of the People and the Pageant-Master of the Revolution. The personal trajectories of the pair converged most dramatically on the day prior to the assassination. David was then serving as president of the Jacobin Club, the extra-parliamentary deliberative body for committed Revolutionaries. This rotating position had just previously been occupied by Marat, but he had lately been out of public view. Worry over his always precarious health, it would seem, led David and a colleague to pay a call, and the artist would later publicly recollect his vivid impression of Marat laboring over his papers while immersed in the kaolin-infused bath that soothed the lesions of his skin ailment.

That vignette of tireless labor stoically endured though pain and deprivation encapsulated the legend to which his passionate following subscribed. He was their vigilant champion, alert to every counter-Revolutionary plot or nefarious scheme to profit from the recurrent shortages of food, ever the fiercest advocate for the wholesale arrest and execution of wrongdoers. While David's pre-Revolutionary prestige and his circle of patronage kept him in relative comfort as his growing political role steadily moved to the Left, Marat's uncompromising intemperance had provoked arrest warrants, police pursuit, and a fugitive's privations during the Revolution's earlier phases. Hardship only added to his aura, while failing to deter the regular appearance of his daily sheet *L'Ami du Peuple.* Even being elected to the Convention after the declaration of the Republic could not prevent his arrest and trial in the spring of 1793 at the behest of equivocating Girondin deputies, enemies of David's Robespierrist faction, the so-called Mountain. By the time of the artist's visit to Marat's austere rooms in the rue des Cordeliers, the two of them concurred as to the radical measures required to protect the honest *sans-culottes* and the Republic itself from the purported machinations of these Girondins. Then, a day later, one of their sympathizers, Charlotte Corday, appeared out of nowhere to confirm every suspicion.

A peak achievement of European painting would follow from that convergence, one that synthesized both the inspiring lights and grim shadows of its historical moment. *Murder in the Rue Marat* proceeds by means of another telling of the French Revolution, as each portion of code in the painting demands an excursus into one more interwoven strand of historical events.[12] There are of course narrative histories of the Revolution beyond counting, but this one at least differs from the rest by allowing David's painting, which was made out of the Revolution, to disclose in the present what it captured and preserved of living experience in 1793.

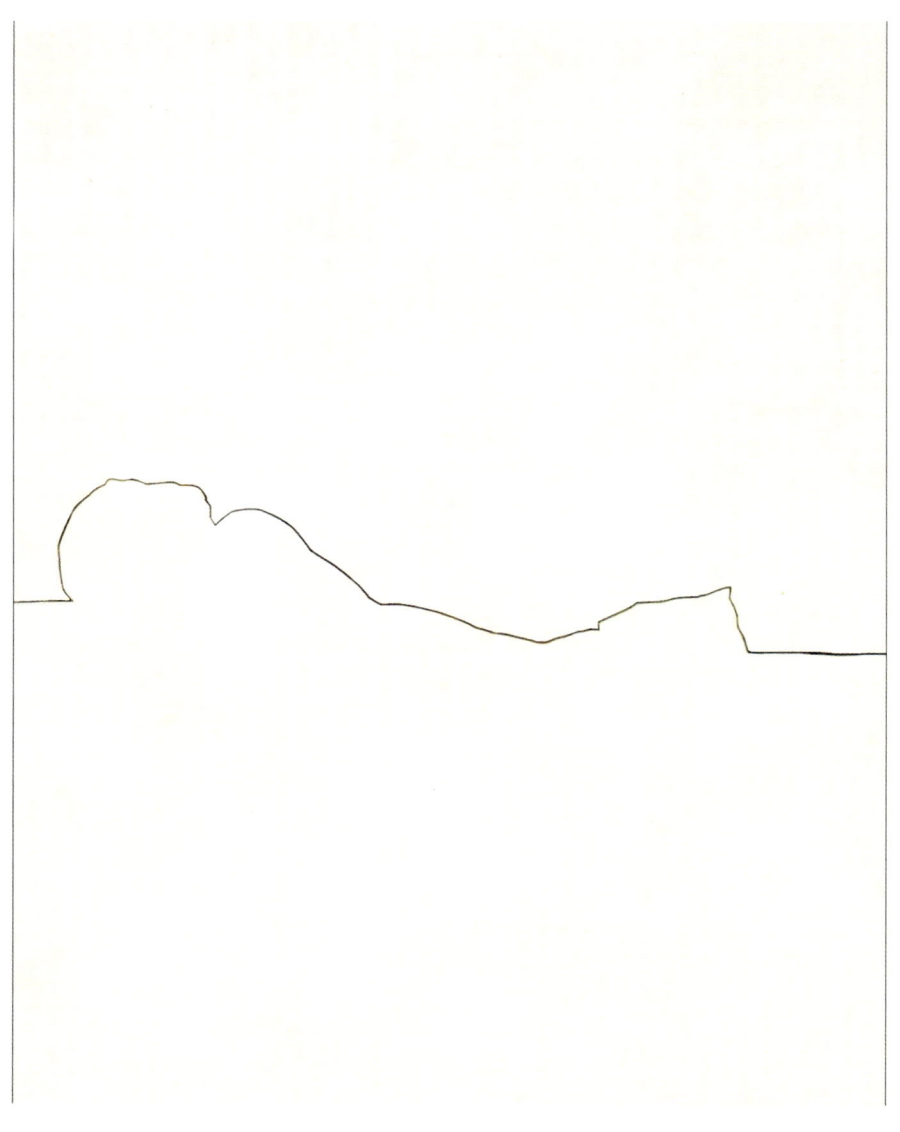

Jacques-Louis David, *Marat at His Last Breath*, 1793, image manipulation by Dominika Ivanická, 2023

2

DIVISION

A WRITTEN NARRATIVE SUCH AS Balzac's *Sarrasine* imposes the order of its apprehension: the reader starts at the beginning and proceeds to the conclusion. Skipping to the end from somewhere in the middle, "to find out what happens," is considered naïve and aberrant, a juvenile cheat on oneself. Obviously enough, no such strictures apply to looking at a painting, where one can look anywhere and in whatever order one pleases. The art of traditional composition consists to a great extent in finding ways to limit this indeterminacy. An artist will draw the viewer's initial attention to features rendered in lighter, warmer, more saturated hues; greater proportionate size and heightened definition work to similar effect. Subordinate areas, to be examined secondarily, will appear dimmed and less distinct, often at the peripheries of the standard rectangle. There are, to be sure, countless ways to modify the formula and confound expectations for effect, but a competent artist will endeavor in some way to guide one's attention in meaningful ways as a counter to the inherent, potentially incorrigible freedom of the viewer's gaze.

The business of verbally describing and characterizing paintings generally proceeds in the manner of a helpful guide conducting a tour around the geography of the canvas, pointing out the prominent landmarks, pathways, territorial boundaries, and historical survivals. Priorities in this guidance should seem sensible but governed by no predetermined system, lest the viewer's recreational experience be constrained. I would hazard that virtually every prior account of David's *Death of Marat*, good, bad, or indifferent, would fall under this heading. So the procedure I had in mind, now as much as in my student days, would need to be distinctly different. Yes, it would necessarily unfold sequentially, but each permutation of the original would comprehend the work as a whole, edge to edge and corner to corner, just under varying stipulations. I have had the good fortune in this endeavor to work with Dominika Ivanická, a student at the Institute of Fine Arts in New York, who realized these modifications with a clarity and imagination that exceeded my prompts to her.

With due regard to Yue Minjun's painting highlighted in the previous chapter—that is, his meticulous re-rendering of David's entire painting with Marat himself extracted from the scene—which of these then should be the first image in this gallery, the first configuration to be isolated from the rest? Once one pulls back from the depicted martyr's ambiguous figure, the most striking characteristic of the painting is arguably the stark contrast between its lower and upper halves. Below the median are found all the items of anatomy and still life parsed in detail by every interpreter of the work. Above it, David provided no more than a barely differentiated field built from short, uniform strokes of his brush. Their darkened hue hovers, for the most part, between brooding greenish grays and browns. Faint illumination seems to increase toward the upper right of the canvas, but no contour, crease, or boundary interrupts the all-over continuity of marks. While some shared tonality with the upper expanse shows up in the shadows below, David made little further effort to signal across the divide. Defying the conventional logic of picture-making, the two halves remain co-dependent but barely reconciled neighbors.

The razor-thin boundary [*page 26*] is the single element shared between the two halves (I asked Ms. Ivanická to make it look like a crack in the ice). But is this implied fissure any more than a left-over artifact of the meeting between the painting's two dominating tectonic plates, such that this first transformation lacks a claim to pictorial substance on a par with everything that falls on either side of it? Absence, nonetheless, assumes a salient presence, in that this division possesses its own provenance, a derivation from the hands of David's devoted if ambivalent pupil, Anne-Louis Girodet, who has already figured in the opening chapter as the author of *The Sleep of Endymion* [*page 18*], the 1791 canvas from which Balzac visualized his androgynous diva in the novella *Sarrasine*. That work was the product of his study years in Rome, his reward for winning the 1789 Grand Prix awarded by the Royal Academy of Painting and Sculpture. Just before departing the next year, the young artist found time to complete a remarkable, enormous *Pietà,* some three-and-a-half meters in height, painted for the church in southwestern France where it still hangs [*page 30*]. This private project gave Girodet the opportunity to stake out independent territory of his own, and he seized the occasion to remake the hallowed devotional motif on his own terms. In place of Christian symbols, he relied on classical or natural attributes: shroud, sarcophagus, cavern, dawn. Risk enough, but compounded by the challenge of making the expanse of virtually featureless cavern wall an effective counterweight to the robustly volumetric lower half. Girodet strikes a note of triumph by carving his signature in a fictive inscription at the foot of the sarcophagus, proudly appending his age of twenty-two.

Just to enumerate these elements of the work is to evoke their obvious parallels in David's *Marat*, but the point of patent convergence between the two lies at their parallel seams between upper zones of shadowy, meditative stillness and lower ones abounding with incident. The most obvious sign of David's reliance on Girodet's *Pietà* appears in the nearly literal tracing of the contour along the head and shoulders of the Virgin. One has only to superimpose a

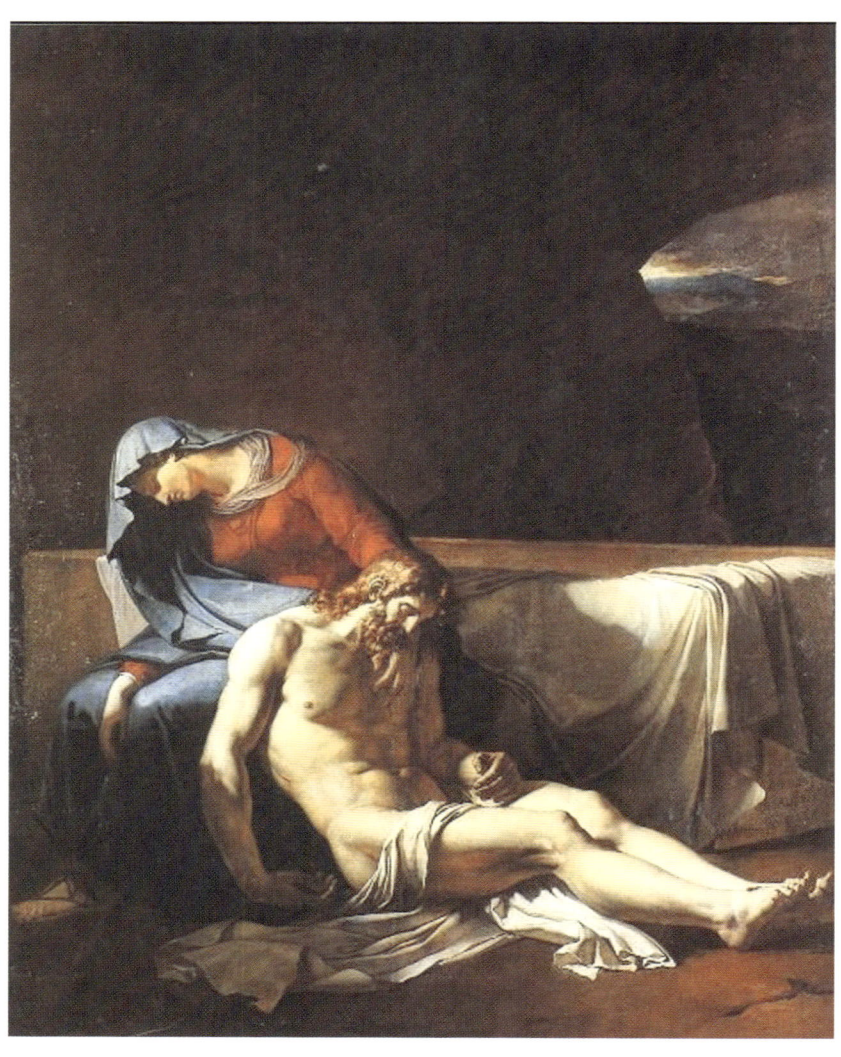

Anne-Louis Girodet, *Pietà*, 1790, oil on canvas, 335 × 235 cm,
Montesquieu-Volvestre, Haute-Garonne, Church of Saint Victor

transparency of David's *Marat* over Girodet's *Pietà* to confirm their correspondence [*below*]. In a startling transposition, the outline of the Virgin has become almost precisely the line of Marat's head and body as they emerge above the bath. The head coverings of Girodet's grieving Mary and David's moribund Marat rise from the horizontal edge of the sarcophagus/bath at the same point and angle, then arc toward their respective shoulders, which coincide almost exactly, as do the upper arms of both figures slanting down toward the rough midpoint, where the horizontal and vertical axes cross. Girodet then carries the boundary line more or less horizontally to where it meets

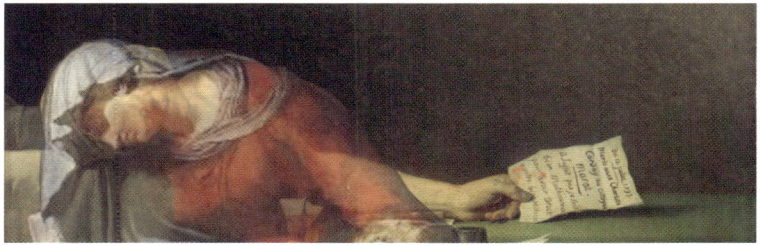

Superimposition of Girodet's *Pietà* over David's *Marat at His Last Breath* (detail), image manipulation by Dominika Ivanická, 2023

the right edge, while David slows that passage with a more complex and decisive contour, using Marat's forearm and the hand holding a duplicitous note Corday had written, but not used, in seeking admission to Marat's bath chamber.

Thus repeated, the seam joining the halves of both paintings transforms itself from idiosyncratic invention in the first instance to a consciously coded element in the second. Out of all the dispersed analogies between the two paintings, it was this formal device that David expressly retained from his pupil's dramatic revision of the Christian devotional formula, as if what he required could be condensed into one abstract line.[1] There would have been nothing out of the ordinary for David to have made or been given some record of this first ambitious, independent work by his star apprentice, but the appropriation would have been legible to few who saw David's *Marat*, as Girodet's painting had been far away from Paris since its completion three years before. It would be hasty, however, to assume that the connection remained a private or negligible matter. François Gérard, who collaborated with David in making the first and best of the *Marat* replicas, had been the closest fellow pupil to Girodet when both were in Paris during 1790. And they had recently been together in Rome, so there would have been at least one informed observer on hand and very likely more within the studio, such that their master would have been addressing a small but significant audience through this explicit act of appropriation and recoding.

As David worked out his composition under the eyes of his studio assistants, what message might those witnesses have been receiving? While the isolated contour cannot yield an answer to that question, nonetheless, it gives rise to a necessary excursion into the particularities of history, not as "context" so much as the full elaboration of this portion of code. Barthes's prose expansions on a given coded passage from Balzac's *Sarrasine* tend to run to no more than a page or two, as these remain within its text-on-text universe. He was many things, but not an historian. Here the historical implications of an isolated pictorial coding, however compressed and parsimonious, will necessarily propel more extended historical excurses. Owing to their non-textual points of departure, their unfolding can depart from customary exposition along more associational paths, though historical logic is in no way meant to suffer in the ensuing, perhaps unexpected joins of topic with topic. So it may be in this first instance: the slightness of the spidery line of division unleashing a paradoxical abundance of implied history off-center from prevailing Revolutionary narratives.

•

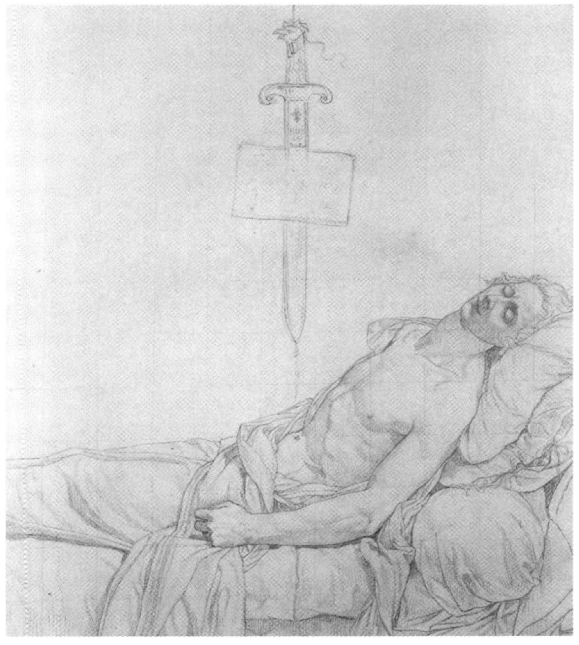

After Jacques-Louis David and François Gérard, *The Death of Lepeletier de Saint-Fargeau.* Drawing by Anatole Devosge, 1793, black chalk on paper, 46.7 × 40 cm, Dijon, Musée des Beaux-Arts

Marat's assassination in mid-July had been preceded in January by the murder of Louis-Michel Lepeletier de Saint-Fargeau, the republican aristocrat and regicide deputy, felled by a sword-wielding ex-royal guardsman at a café in the Palais-Royal in retaliation for voting in favor of the execution of Louis XVI. In honor of this martyr, David had already carried out the duties that Marat's death would later demand of him: arranging for a funeral procession and lying in state, along with fashioning a commemorative portrait (now lost) to be hung behind the speakers in the legislative chamber [*above*]. Just a week before

Lepeletier's death, however, another Revolutionary, Nicolas-Jean Hugou de Bassville, had likewise been assassinated, though to considerably less notice. Bassville had died in Rome, while functioning at the time as de facto French envoy to the papal seat—but only if that title were to imply unremitting defiance and hostility toward his host. The Royal Academy of Painting and Sculpture had lost its patron with the forced abdication of Louis XVI the previous August, leaving its outpost in Rome, prominently positioned in Palazzo Mancini on the Corso, to serve as Bassville's base of operations. As such, it became the most visible target for a Roman populace whipped by churchmen into violent antagonism toward the heretical French polity. The removal of all royal symbols from the edifice of the former Royal Academy had escalated the conflict, which came to a head when the remaining students, led by Girodet, painted a standing warrior goddess as a republican symbol to serve in their place.

On 13 January 1793, Bassville was waylaid by a mob in the Corso, pursued into a temporary refuge, and brutally murdered. The small number of former students left in the old Academy nearby, as they worked furiously to complete the new figurehead of the Republic, became a convenient target. Girodet later recounted the events in a letter to his foster father, which reads, in part:

> We were no more than four at the Academy, and we still had our brushes in our hands when the furious rabble burst in and instantly reduced the doors, windows, and glass to dust, as well as all the statues on the stairways and in the apartments. They had but twenty steps to mount before they could assassinate us; we spared them the effort by moving more quickly than they did. These wretches were so besotted with destruction that they didn't even notice us; but soldiers, who proved to be executioners almost equal to the ones we had feared, far from con-

fronting them, made us descend more than a hundred steps under the blows of their rifle butts before we could reach the street, where we found ourselves abandoned and without any help in the middle of this rabble thirsting for our blood . . . One of my comrades was pursued by a rain of paving stones; I fled the thrusts of knives. The tortuous streets and our cool heads saved us for the moment. Escaping this danger and believing that I was taking sound precautions, I ran to Bassville's house at the very moment of his assassination . . . I ducked into an Italian house a few steps away and stayed inside until nightfall. I was foolhardy enough then to return to the Academy, which had become the Palace of Priam. The mob was ready to break down the doors with an axe and to put it to the torch.[2]

He reports that a former model lent protection to him and a companion, enabling their escape to Naples, where the French maintained a bastion. There he waited on events, ill with malaria likely contracted on his southward flight through the marshes, afterwards slowly making his way back to France via Venice, but too deliberately to be present for Marat's assassination in July and the turbulent struggle between the Republican factions that preceded it.

The absent Girodet, nonetheless, would have maintained a presence in his teacher's thoughts. In March 1793, David urgently sought his pupil's address in Naples, having successfully intervened with the ruling Committee of Public Safety to have money forwarded there. That anxiety might well have been heightened by the memory of his own role in the plight of his pupil. Prior to the attack on Bassville and the pillaging of the former Academy, David had demanded, brooking no delay, an *"auto-da-fé"* of royal symbols and statuary at the Roman Academy, defying prudent advice that such Republican provocations would leave the students on the ground exposed to unnecessary danger.[3]

Over the course of June, despite his continued absence, Girodet became the closest thing to an activist-hero among artists that the young Republic had known. That month, an enterprising journalist calling himself Michel de Cubières published a pamphlet under the title *The Death of Bassville or the Conspiracy of Pius VI Unmasked*.[4] Though a titled aristocrat by birth, Cubières (or Dorat-Cubières) had been putting himself forward as an enthusiastic Jacobin publicist, while assuming office as a prosecutor in the Commune of Paris, the body formed by the forty-eight local districts of Paris where the *sans-culotte* activists were directly represented. Just how closely his Bassville account aligned itself with Girodet's personal interests and image is signaled in its opening words, "You know, my dear master . . . ," at which point an asterisk directs the reader to this explanatory note:

> This is not the author who is speaking, but a young French artist, a pupil of David, a resident of Rome at the time of Bassville's murder, and an eyewitness to the facts that he will relate. The author believed it appropriate to render this account in the first person in his voice in order to lend to the narration greater fluency, vividness, and fire.

The "dear master" is plainly David, to whom the pamphlet is addressed as an imaginary letter. Cubières, the would-be voice of the radical Revolution, assumes Girodet's identity in providing the first extended narrative available to ordinary Parisians of the January riots in Rome in such a way that it became the young artist's own story.

Cubières's extended account of all the events involved in Bassville's appearance on the Roman scene keeps itself to Girodet's voice. When crafting his committedly political persona in letters to intimates six months before, he was unlikely to have anticipated its being now so prodigiously amplified and embellished in public print. Cooperation between artist and publicist must surely have existed, even if the former's precise contribution to the intransigent identity that Cubières created for him remains unclear. But their joint effort caused him decisively to stand out from his artist contemporaries, sharing the risks of Bassville if not his fate. Cubières wraps his story around the painting of the goddess personifying the Republic, responsibility for which he gives entirely to the hero of his text. In a key scene, Girodet is challenged by hostile Romans, to whom he replies with heedless provocation: "so it is you then, they said to me with harsh irony, who should make this marvelous figure. Yes, it was I, vile slaves, unworthy of the name of Roman, which you have disgraced and made an object of contempt for peoples everywhere; yes, it was none other than I, and know that if I tried to paint it, I would know still better how to defend it."

If Girodet in the end found it impossible to make good his boast, Cubières's retelling gives him full marks for bravery in the face of the overwhelming numbers and ferocity of the rioters who invaded the Palazzo Mancini—and presumably tore to pieces the figure of Republican Liberty as its young creators fled for their lives. A matter of weeks after the appearance of *The Death of Bassville,* of course, everything changed with the most incendiary assassination of the Revolution, overwhelming whatever belated outrage Cubières had managed to provoke over Bassville's martyrdom. While Marat's demise would have eclipsed public consciousness of the envoy's ultimate sacrifice, it conversely could have sharpened David's private focus on Girodet's example, both in life and on canvas.

The logic of David's portrait condensed itself inside the borrowed dividing contour and all the drama of martyrdom and mourning it implied. Was it a tribute of solidarity with a valorous absent comrade, one who had acted on the master's exhortations and paid the price when the reactionaries struck back? Or was it a domination performance, asserting that what is yours will always be mine? Either as a gift or a prize, Girodet's line saved David a great deal of trouble

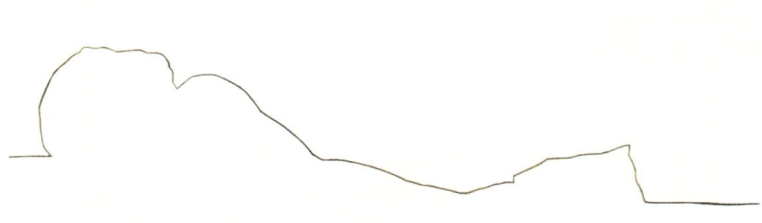

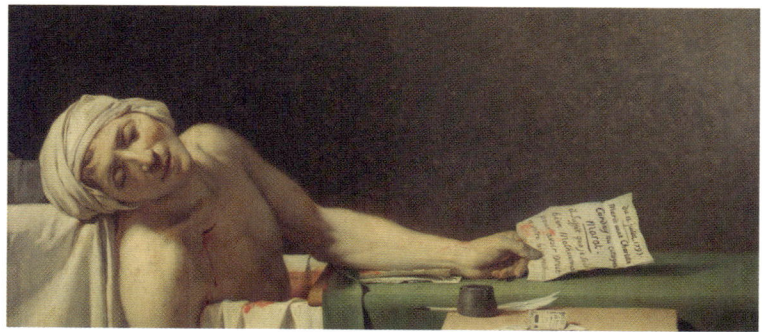

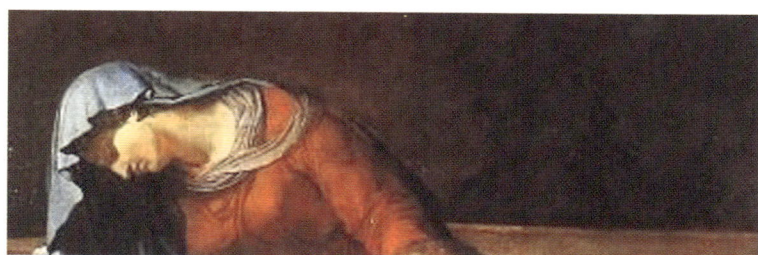

Details from: (*top*) Jacques-Louis David, *Marat at His Last Breath*, 1793,
image manipulation by Dominika Ivanická, 2023; (*center*) Jacques-Louis David, *Marat at His Last Breath* (detail), 1793, oil on canvas, Brussels, Royal Museums of Belgium;
(*bottom*) Anne-Louis Girodet, *Pietà* (detail), 1790, oil on canvas,
Montesquieu-Volvestre, Haute-Garonne, Church of Saint Victor

in finding an arrestingly fresh memorialization of the ostentatiously austere and extreme Friend of the People, a striking departure from the routine dead-classical-hero-on-a-bier that had sufficed for Lepeletier. The character of the line intimates a jagged scar left by a wound, the suturing of which stitches together David's composition, dividing and uniting at the same time. In Girodet's painting, the largely featureless wall of the rock tomb yields in the upper right to a dawn sky; his upper zone thus stands in a literal scriptural sense for the future, but more deeply instantiates the Christian concept of Christ's redemption dividing human history into an incommensurable before and after. The suture between the coming realm of light (upper zone) and passing mortal existence (lower zone) henceforth just barely holds, with all worldly bodies and things now destined for oblivion in the Last Days. Both of Girodet's figures will exit the earth much sooner, of course, each to be bodily lifted into the afterlife. By contrast, David's repetition had all of its work to do in this fallen, carnal world. So it is to the corporeal dimension of his painting that the next chapter must turn.

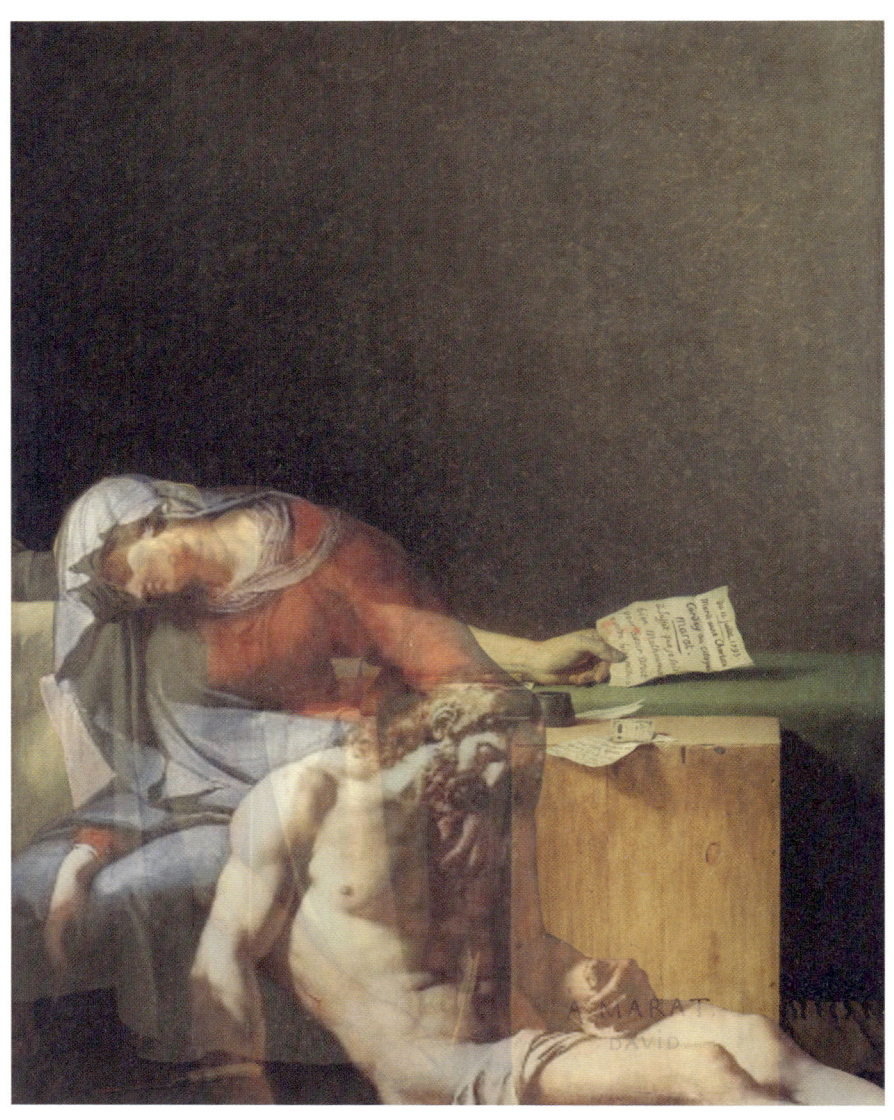

Superimposition of Girodet's *Pietà* over David's *Marat at His Last Breath*,
image manipulation by Dominika Ivanická, 2023

3

FUSION

The observable dependence of Jacques-Louis David's renowned *Death of Marat* on the little-known *Pietà* by his pupil Anne-Louis Girodet has been slow to sink in among the art commentariat. One exception has been the philosopher Rebecca Comay, who has embraced the connection with a flourish. In the course of David's assimilation of Girodet's prototype, she writes, "The figures of Christ and Virgin, corpse and mother, momentarily coalesce. In the inky shadows of the tomb Marat embraces himself, completes the circuit of his own *Pietà*, becomes his own progenitor and survivor, at once son and mother to himself. Self-mourning, self-engendering, both preceding and succeeding himself, perpetually giving birth to himself, like a phoenix."[1] Comay shifts the register from Christian to pagan in the last line, befitting the earthly destiny of Marat's remains. She also understands the artist not to have actually excised the female antagonist from the scene, but to have instead melded male and female together, whereby, as Comay puts it, "Marat embraces himself, completes the circuit of his own *Pietà*."

Implied in this striking formulation is the subsuming of the female into what we see of the male protagonist, which the second of Dominika Ivanická's manipulations vividly manifests [*facing page*]. As noted in the previous chapter, the Virgin Mary supplies the shape of her head and shoulders to those of the secular martyr, who is

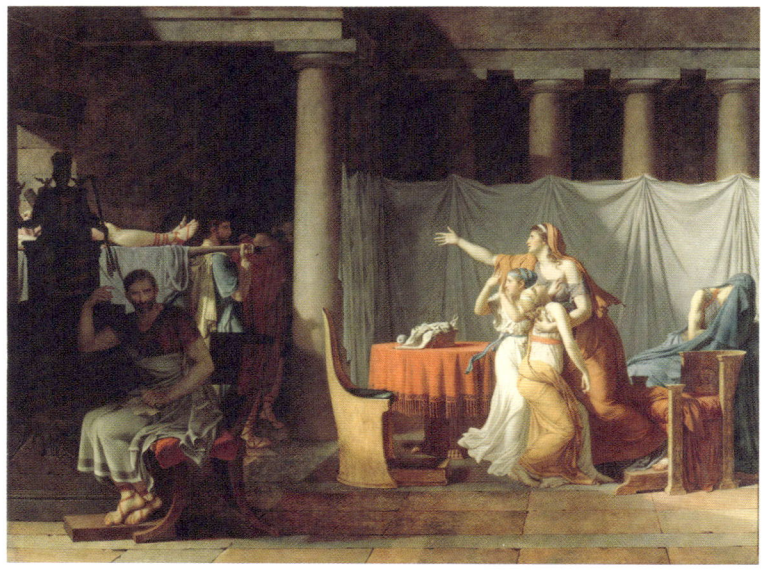

above and facing page   Jacques-Louis David, *The Lictors Bringing to Brutus the Bodies of His Sons*, 1789, oil on canvas, 323 × 422 cm, Paris, Musée du Louvre

furnished with the right arm displaced upward from the slumping body of her son, the divine sacrifice and scapegoat for the sins of humanity. The rest of the Christ's exposed body is simply remaindered out, leaving David's identikit selection and reassembly of Girodet's components as significantly female as it is male. The Virgin's downcast profile has been overlaid with Marat's full-face portrait, which entailed at least three reversals, one in orientation, a second in gender, and a third in status from mourner to mourned. As relationships go, reversal is as strong if not stronger than replication, more decisive and requiring greater motivation. And Girodet's Virgin had already arisen from another reversal, one taken from the tragic and monumental *Lictors Bringing to Brutus the Bodies of His Sons*, unveiled in the Revolutionary summer of 1789 [*facing page*].

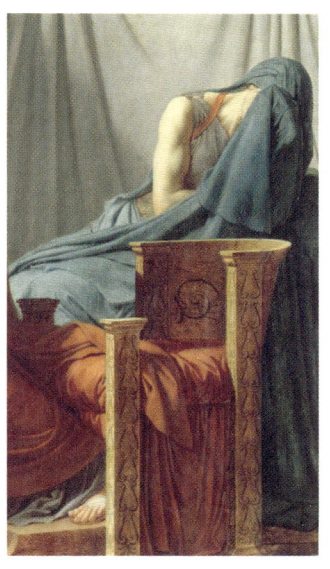

The unbending consul, founder of the Roman republic, has been compelled to put his male heirs to death for their treasonous violation of laws that he himself wrote. In contrast to the equivocal expression of Brutus, seated at the far left with his back to the procession bearing his sons' bodies, their aged nurse at the opposite end of the composition buries her face in her cloak, manifesting the supreme expression of grief as codified in antiquity (that is, sorrow so profound that it exceeds the descriptive capacities of painting). If David's *Marat* owed Girodet a profound debt, here indebtedness had flowed the other way, as the master entrusted another pupil, François Gérard, with the entire execution of this key figure, perhaps the finest moment in the painting as a whole. Girodet then borrowed the contour of the nurse's head and shoulders in reversed orientation for his grieving Mary of the following year.

Does David's duplication of that outline in Marat's silhouette then perform the pagan-to-Christian transformation in reverse? An answer to that question is less clear, as it depends on how secular the *Marat* painting is taken to be, a perennial and unresolved argument. A chief exhibit for those discounting Christian connotations has been a vivid exchange recorded at the left-wing Cordeliers club, Marat's erstwhile headquarters, two weeks after the assassination. An orator waxed at length on the analogy between the Revolutionary martyr and Christ, stressing their common frugality, tender generosity to the poor, and detestation of hypocritical priests, financial swindlers, and the rich in general: "Oh sacred heart of Jesus, Oh sacred heart of Marat," he intoned.[2] But the analogy drew a sharp retort from a *sans-culotte* named Brochet, who then mounted the tribune to rule out any more such talk. From this Christ, he countered, had descended "the seeds of fanaticism and all the senseless drivel that have disfigured Liberty from the day he was born." Reinforcing this rejoinder would have been the fact that Brochet had been tasked by the club with finding a suitably honorific container for the preservation of Marat's heart.

The prevailing Republican doctrine of de-Christianization would appear to confirm Brochet's position; but it largely failed to carry the day, as the political complications of that moment worked to undermine anti-clerical zeal. Robespierre, from his commanding position on the Committee of Public Safety, opposed the wholesale suppression of Christian monuments and ceremony, leaving no one in doubt as to his abhorrence of the atheism that followed from the rhetoric of the more vehement among the de-Christianizers. And external events counseled circumspection, as there had raged a Catholic-inspired revolt centered in the western region of the Vendée since early in the spring of 1793. This uprising ignited savage clashes between quasi-guerilla peasant bands and units of the National Guard, the zone of conflict expanding eastward through the Loire Valley, which is to say into the heart of France. These incursions coincided with secular opposition mounting from multiple directions, amplifying the dangers of provoking more religiously infused resistance.

Prominent citizens in a large proportion of the nation's commercial centers were going so far as to mobilize local populations to march on Paris and put an end to the current Jacobin leadership. The merchant and manufacturing elite of Lyon, the nation's second city, successfully forged an alliance with counterparts (*fédérés*) in the southern ports of Marseille and Toulon, with the latter even opening itself on 2 September to occupation by the enemy English and surrendering its portion of the national fleet. These internal threats were unfolding against the backdrop of military turmoil on the northeastern frontier. Like the marquis de Lafayette the previous summer, the succeeding, nobly born French commander Charles-François Dumouriez had first attempted to march his troops against the Convention in Paris. When they mutinied at his orders, he had likewise gone over to the enemy in an act of massive betrayal. Edicts from the Convention ordering forced recruitment to stem these losses, the levée of 300,000 as it was called, fueled widespread regional rebellions, particularly where devotion to Catholicism ran highest.

All the while, the new republican Constitution had been hanging fire as it underwent ratification by the assemblies across the country. Even with the success of that formal process in June, Robespierre and his fellow Montagnards had reason to fear, in the face of internal turmoil, the effective nullification of the new national order—a further strong reason for treading lightly where traditional religious sensibilities were in play. David's adoption of a religious template for his Marat painting would thus have entailed no lack of imagination on his part, no inability to generate a fresh paradigm: it was precisely what was required. The chilly classicism of his memorial to the martyred Lepeletier could not have satisfied the brief implicit in the calculations of the leadership. And all the better if its deepest debts to religious art came in disguise, so as not to put off allies among the *sans-culottes* who shared Brochet's jaundiced view of Catholic superstition.

Even before he could put brush to canvas, David naturally orchestrated the funeral ceremonies for Marat, something of a real-world rehearsal for his composition. An analogously pantheistic religiosity suited the occasion, though there was little of the heavenward in the way that David arranged Marat's corpse for the procession and burial three days after his assassination. He did his best to present Marat in the attitude he had last witnessed in life. The surgeon who took charge of the body embalmed all of it except the head and chest so that these parts would, it was hoped, appear more natural with the corpse arranged on a plain bed, naked to the waist with gaping chest wound exposed. Onlookers nonetheless witnessed, from the first lying in state of Marat's body to the procession that coiled through the streets of the Left Bank, a barely intact, visibly deteriorating body. Every account highlights the oppressively hot July weather that accelerated the putrefaction of the corpse, such that no embalming or incense could mask the odor. The discolored skin of the deceased had to be slathered with white makeup, while the descending right arm, arranged by David as he would do in the painting, had so detached itself from the torso that the attending surgeon was obliged to sew it more securely into place.

It appears no coincidence that rumors sprang up, fanned by opportunistic right-wing voices, that plague had arrived in the capital.[3] The historian Jacques Gilhaumou observes a marked change in the rhetoric of orators in the late hours of 16 July, as the march paused at rostra set up in places of public assembly like the place Saint-Michel and the place du Théâtre Français (the Odéon). Those speaking did their best to draw attention away from the rotting corpse, seizing more and more on the compensatory formula "Marat is not dead," that promise waxing as the physical body waned. The procession concluded at the former convent of the Cordeliers [*facing page*], meeting place of the so-named radical club, directly across from the building where Marat had lived. The complex possessed a garden, and under its trees the body was interred (with only the heart held back for preservation). As fearsome a character as Pierre-Gaspard Chaumette, the prosecutor for the Commune of Paris, declared, "Under a tree is where Marat, man of Nature, must be buried. That is our Pantheon." A subsequent report by the Commune expanded poetically on "the trembling leaves reflecting and multiplying the gentle light."[4]

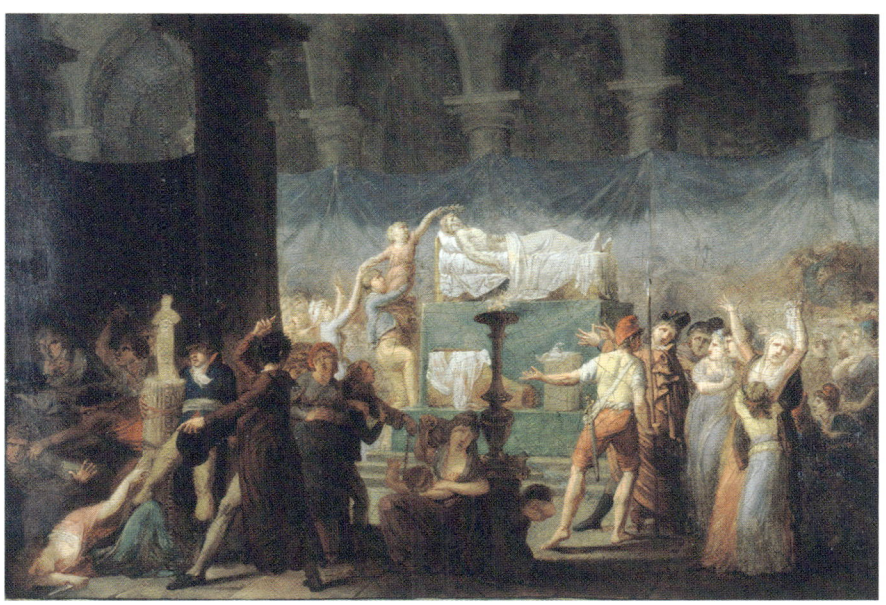

Attributed to Fougeat, *Funeral Ceremony of Marat in the Former Church of the Cordeliers, 15 and 16 July 1793*, oil on canvas, 59 × 73 cm, Paris, Musée Carnavalet

Almost from the moment of the murder, the street outside had become the gathering place for Marat's mourners and therefore provided the site where their collective emotions had been evolving. Among them, feelings over the proper destination for Marat's remains became a source of contention. The Pantheon, the massive former church of Sainte-Geneviève repurposed as a shrine to the nation's official heroes, had immediately been mooted as their suitably honorific repository. But that sentiment soon gave way to the contemptuous dismissal of that destination, the consensus shifting to the view that it would be unworthy of the martyr. Not only did the prior bestowal of that honor on a perceived traitor like Mirabeau compromise the venue, its architectural pomp alone offended their egalitarian presumptions. Yes, a Pantheon, they argued, but far better a "natural Pantheon," collectively carried in the hearts of all those who cherished his memory and sought to realize his convictions, a resting place vastly more imposing and honorific than any mere edifice of stone. In the words of one Jacobin orator, "Everywhere Marat will be, there will be our Pantheon."[5]

•

If transfigured nature were to be the scene of Marat's restoration to wholeness, David would have had difficulty, for his own purposes, banishing from his thoughts the unadorned grotto in which Girodet had staged his *Pietà*. He, of course, did no such thing, not only for the sake of naturalizing Marat's painted place of rest, but equally to answer the primary challenge facing him—that is, how to evoke the two female agents essential to the facts of the event, both of whom gripped the popular imagination. First in moral priority would have been Simone Evrard, Marat's longtime, staunchly protective companion. Her loyalty and steadfastness formed a vital supplement to the Marat legend, especially for the large numbers of female activists who formed groups keeping vigil outside the victim's residence. In that David insisted on his portrait capturing Marat "at his last breath," his subject's reported final exhalation consisted of a choked outcry to her as his chest filled with blood: "A moi, à moi, ma chère amie, je me meurs!" She had run to throw herself upon him in a vain effort to staunch the wound, so the time of the painting suspends itself just before her desperate entrance—and by implication just after Corday had been seized by the assistant who had been folding news sheets in the adjoining room.

In so far as the slumping Marat was evocative of Christ, Evrard could readily provide an implicit substitute for the grieving Virgin, comparable in her reputation for selfless devotion and celebrated for having enveloped her companion in her arms, Pietà-like, at the moment of his death. But the physical presence of Charlotte Corday could not for a moment escape the thoughts of his contemporaneous viewers. The domestic character of the Marat-Evrard bond, moreover, for all of its calamitous ending, lacked the charge of difference commensurate with the force required to compress Girodet's biblical pair so forcefully into David's single entity. If Marat was to become, as Rebecca Comay so eloquently articulates, "his own progenitor and survivor, at once son and mother to himself. Self-mourning, self-engendering, both preceding and succeeding himself," a more heightened, energetically charged dyad was called for, one with equivalent *terribilità* on either side. If truly at his last breath, given that Marat died almost instantly from the knife of his assailant, where has she gone? Where are the signs of disruption that would have followed from her presence, even if just out of frame? Apart from the unrealistically discreet wound to the chest, the only clue to the crime to be seen is the knife dropped to the floor at the lower left, with its blood-stained blade and handle (a kitchen implement she had bought that day and carried tucked next to her own chest in its cardboard covering). Other residues left from Corday's lethal intrusion litter the scene (to receive their due consideration in the chapters that follow). But she figures in more pervasive if non-literal form by virtue of her reputed vitality's contrasting so vividly with Marat's already moribund condition, as repulsive to view, in the eyes of many, before death as afterward.

Since Marat had first taken to the public stage on his election as deputy to the National Convention in September 1792, accounts of his physical appearance tested the prevailing rhetoric of revulsion. One "ally" among the *conventionnels* speaks of his first encounter: "I considered him with the uneasy curiosity one would feel in contemplating certain hideous insects. His disheveled clothes, livid face, and haggard eyes carried something repellant and dreadful that afflicted his soul."[6] By contrast, Corday's proudly calm demeanor, even on her way to the scaffold and atop it, commanded admiring commentary, even from some who abhorred her crime. According to one erotically smitten witness, her poise survived even a drenching downpour on the approach to the guillotine: "She was superb in her long red dress that clung to her body in the rain. One would have thought her a statue, so calm were her features. Behind the wagon, girls held hands and danced. For at least eight days I was in love with Charlotte Corday."[7] As might be expected, Jacobin-aligned writers, having etherealized Marat into an avatar of benevolent Nature, depicted Corday as the opposite: un-natural and outside of womankind in every respect. The departmental authority in Paris, alarmed by all the encomia on Corday's behalf, distributed a circular reading in part: "This woman, whom they call so beautiful, was nothing but a virago . . . hard, insolent, common, and covered in hives . . . shameless and immodest . . . arousing only disgust and repulsion."[8]

There is a mirroring convergence between such negative descriptions of Corday—derived from the subtraction of every attractive trait advanced in praise of the assassin—and the living Marat's actual appearance, down to her being "covered in hives." That portrayal more resembled the sinewy, vengeful persona that her victim had cultivated in life, the deputy who regularly wore a brace of pistols into the Convention. Both that fierce Marat and his rebarbative Corday counterpart could then be removed from David's composition as equal and opposite values, allowing for David's compression of both the positive female and male remainders into one figure. Corday's retained traits of vitality, composure, and self-possession thus migrate into and invigorate the depleted male subject, such that he appears more vigorous at the moment of death than he had lately been in life. As Helen Weston observes, the assassin's absence "served both to conjure her up as hidden menace and simultaneously to leave the qualities of courage and beauty with Marat, together with a suggestion of a miraculous healing of his 'leprous' condition."[9] Arriving at a similar recognition, J.-R. Mantion takes rhetorical flight: "Marat (father, son, Christ, pen holder, soul) *is* Charlotte ('virago,' inscribed woman, death, wing, 'hint of tenderness,' as well as the soul of the entire arrangement). Each personage, both presented and represented, like each object, occupies in turn the place of the other."[10]

David had been one exception among the *conventionnels* on the Left in cultivating a friendship with Marat rather than averting his gaze (another was Augustin Robespierre, brother of the leader).[11] A sympathetic bond might have arisen from their shared abnormalities, Marat's skin inflammation matched by David's tumorous growth on one cheek, which distorted his face and slurred his speech. Their relationship makes the artist's visit to his friend on the day before his murder less fortuitous than it might otherwise seem, as it likewise helps explain, beyond propagandistic requirements, his zeal to show the victim in the most benign light. Even amid the complicated preparations for the 10 August Festival of Unity, being staged to welcome the new constitution on the first anniversary of the Republic's founding, he found the time to render Marat's face in death with great care. The life-sized portrait head, meticulously rendered on paper, already strives to show the martyr to best advantage [*page 52*]. But that relative improvement only emphasizes the extent of cross-gender modification required to achieve the seraphic countenance that shines forth from the painting, manifestly evident when turning the detail of the head to a comparably upright position [*page 53*]. By virtue of that transfer, the martyr's skin clears, muscle tone and subcutaneous fat firm up, cheeks and eyelids fill out, the latter assuming almond proportions, as if expanded with collagen injections. The vinegar-soaked linen over his scalp assumes the air of the fashionably informal headwrap on one of Elisabeth Vigeé-Lebrun's period female sitters. Marat was fifty at the time of his death and surely graying, but the russet locks that escape the wrap appear

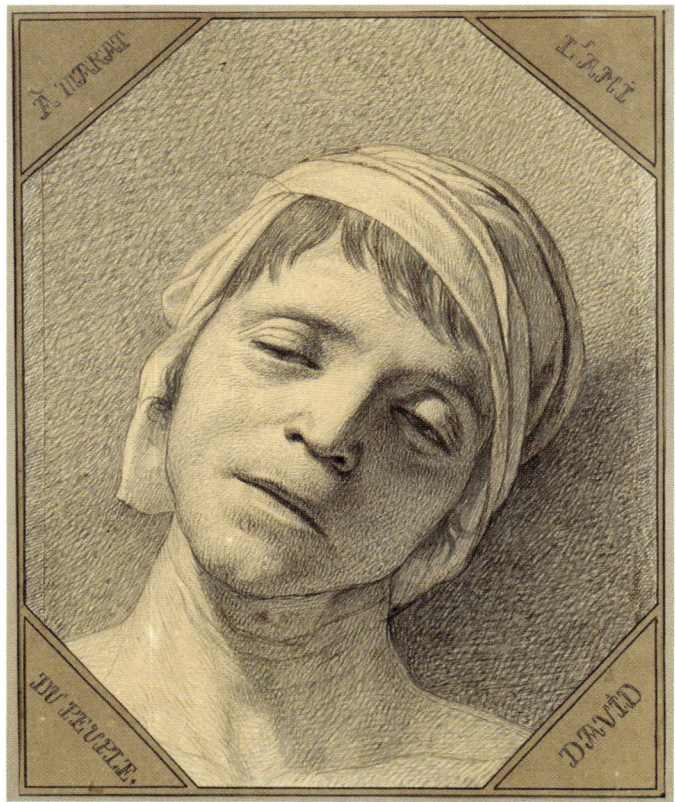

Jacques-Louis David, *Head of Marat*, 1793, ink on white paper pasted
onto a brown background. 27cm × 21 cm, Versailles Collections

positively coquettish. The often-remarked androgyny of David's
Marat arose systematically from the splitting Corday had under-
gone in the public imagination, her doubling into imaginary good
and bad twins. The cloud of traits to which she owed her outward
allure could then be set free and reassigned to the otherwise un-
presentable Marat, returning him to wholeness while leaving behind

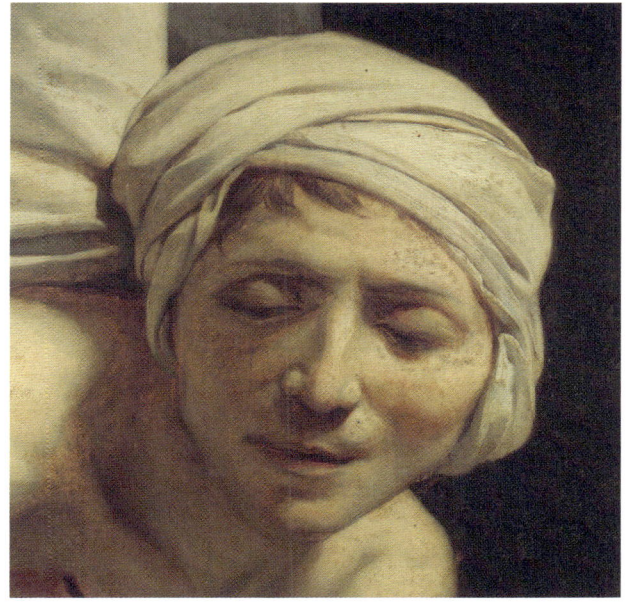

Jacques-Louis David, *Marat at His Last Breath*, 1793, oil on canvas,
165 × 182 cm, Brussels, Royal Museums of Belgium (detail, rotated 90°)

as an implicit residue the female monster whose repellant outward
aspect matched the depravity of her crime and the danger of her
associations.

•

Corday's associations comprised Marat's most determined enemies,
the so-called Girondins. That faction of deputies owed this sobri-
quet to the region around Bordeaux, the Gironde, home to a number
of their group. They inclined in general toward the interests and

outlook of France's peripheral commercial centers, one reason for the prominence of ports and trading cities in the Federalist revolt (and for their foot-dragging over the abolition of profitable slavery in the colonies). Marat's allies in the Mountain, by contrast, drew a preponderance of adherents from northern regions centered on Paris, with legal pleading a predominant pursuit. The Girondins had been the party of war from the start, while many unconvinced Montagnards came from areas occupied by the enemy during the seesaw movements of the northeastern front. While the actual differences between these two sets of bourgeois politicos had not initially been acute, the pervasive fears of invasion and betrayal over the course of 1792, exacerbated by mounting suspicions and mutual recriminations, had come to widen them beyond hope of reconciliation.

One of the most decisive errors made by the Girondins arose from their particular antipathy toward Marat, which led them to revoke his parliamentary immunity in April 1793 and drive his prosecution for perceived incitements to extra-legal violence. His subsequent acquittal before the Revolutionary Tribunal in May, cheered on by a vociferous claque of *sans-culotte* supporters, turned the tables, with his antagonists finding themselves fatally open to legal pursuit in return. While their Montagnard colleagues in the Convention were not yet inclined to take retaliatory measures, all doubts were overtaken by more decisive initiatives emanating from the Paris Commune, headquartered toward the east at the old city hall (l'Hôtel de Ville), channeling angry *sans-culotte* demands that twenty-two deputies of the Gironde be surrendered and placed under arrest. Marat, though himself a *conventionnel*, had a strong hand in this, playing both sides of the street in what would be his last public hurrah.

On the heels of their overreach over Marat, further missteps by the Girondins played into the hands of their popular enemies. One of their number, Maximin Isnard, foolishly issued a notorious threat

to the entire city, founded on the illusion that his faction commanded the allegiance of the nation. Should they be harmed, "Paris
will be annihilated. Soon men will walk on the banks of the Seine
and wonder if a city ever existed."[12] Still in nominal control of the
Convention, Isnard's allies pushed through a measure establishing
a body called the Commission of Twelve, its appointees charged
with investigating and pursuing the militants. The abolition of this
entity became a further cause for the deliberately planned insurrection, which began unfolding on 29 May and persisted for nearly a
week, with tocsins, secret meetings, and street gatherings going on
around the clock. At its peak, a ring of some 4,000 Commune troops,
backed up by 80,000 more, as well as waiting batteries of cannon,
surrounded the Convention's meeting place in the Tuileries Palace.[13]
Had a delegation of Montagnards not bravely fraternized with this
virtual army, the Convention itself might have been violently dispersed. But its hand had, nonetheless, been forced, and a majority
of deputies voted for the charges against their erstwhile Girondin
colleagues as treasonous plotters against "the unity and indivisibility
of the Republic." Another principal at the insurrectionary Commune
was Michel de Cubières, then completing his celebratory account of
Girodet's actions in Rome discussed in the previous chapter. Where
Girodet had fled for his life before the reactionary Roman mob in January, Cubières did his part in launching this popular campaign that
ensured the triumph of the Left in Paris (thus lending an insurgent
topicality to his account of Girodet's exploits, published a matter of
days later).

Even the more left-leaning deputies, however, resented the impla-
cable pressure from the Commune and the popular sections to move
against the Girondins, along with the various humiliations they had
themselves endured in the process. Lax treatment of the proscribed
former colleagues likely followed from this anger, many rightly
fearing that following through at the behest of the militants could

inaugurate a cycle of preemptive retribution that could eventually put all of them in jeopardy. The Montagnard leadership, now firmly in control, contented itself at first with placing the accused under loose house arrest, with its primary attention directed toward the roll-out of the new constitution, hurried forward in order to provide a focus for unity after the recent upheavals.[14] It was not so much the (real) dangers posed by the accused Girondins as it was the energized popular movement that attracted official vigilance, especially where the proposed constitutional provisions were concerned. The activist ex-priest Jacques Roux, with a following in the artisanal Gravilliers section of the Haut-Marais, denounced the document, in a petition to the Convention, for its lack of any provision banning hoarding, monopolies, and speculation in grain.[15] By so breaking the façade of common purpose, he made himself a compensatory target for the Montagnards, who were otherwise constrained from chastening the *sans-culottes*.

Not only was Roux immediately and roundly denounced by Robespierre, he also found himself on the outs with Marat, whom he would have counted a kindred spirit. When a phalanx of Montagnards, led by Robespierre, trooped to the Cordeliers club to demand Roux's expulsion, they read out a letter from Marat himself echoing Robespierre's denunciation of the "Red Priest" as a false patriot serving the divisive interests of France's foreign enemies. Seeking to escape his predicament, Roux in early July sought out Marat at home, just four days in advance of Corday, but found no relief from l'Ami du Peuple, who loudly castigated him once more as a counter-revolutionary Tartuffe.[16]

While all of this was going on, the expelled Girondin deputies began surreptitiously slipping away from their confinement to filter into the provinces, many into the orbit of the Federalist revolt. Corday would come from the Norman city of Caen, where nine of the fugitives had fled, moving into quarters across the street from her house. A keen follower of political events and republican by conviction, the twenty-four-year-old fell in in with their plans to raise a force to march on the capital and suppress the radicalism embodied by Marat, such that she conceived a self-sacrificing role for herself as personal avenger. Resigned to her own death, she had conscientiously put her affairs in order before leaving Caen, bearing a letter of introduction to another Girondin in Paris. Once there, she first searched for Marat at one of his old haunts in the Palais Royal, then at the Convention, until she discovered his lying low at home and improvised her plan to gain an audience.

All of this Corday frankly and calmly revealed under interrogation, her testimony seeming to confirm a conspiracy and turning the Girondin dispute with the Mountain into a matter of life and death on both sides (as so it transpired). If more proof were needed, on the very day of Marat's murder, the insurrectionary Federalist force from Caen, egged on by the fugitive Girondins, had managed to march as far as the valley of the Seine just to the west of Paris. That underwhelming sally found itself summarily checked by the patriot National Guard with not one casualty. Though handily defeated, yet another head of the Federalist hydra had revealed itself, its emissary this uncanny female assassin. The two events were even more closely entwined, as the uninspiring muster of this force a week before had so dismayed Corday that she rightly despaired over its prospects, resolving to step into the breach herself.[17]

Following the murder, the ruling deputies came to believe all the more that the fates of Lepeletier and Marat could await them at any moment. Roux found himself hauled before the Police Committee to answer suspicions of complicity—a bitter turn of events for someone who had for years gloried in his alternative nickname, "le petit Marat." Once exonerated, Roux wasted no time reviving the old title of his namesake's journal, styling himself now as "the ghost of Marat." Robespierre however, was having none of it and in August brought before the Convention no less a witness than the sainted Simone Evrard, who denounced all the pretenders purporting to make the spirit of her martyred companion speak, "in order to outrage his memory and mislead the people."[18] That hammer blow to the credibility of the so-called *Enragés* around Roux came two days before the 10 August celebrations prepared by David in the name, above all else, of the national unity. Those plans, however, inadvertently exacerbated the threat to its achievement that the likes of Roux were taken to pose.

In addition to its marking the first anniversary of the monarchy's fall, the 10 August Festival was intended to seal the successful ratification of the new constitution, submitted since June to popular votes in all the cantons across the country. The cantonal representatives, many of them young, traveled to Paris to deliver their affirmative local tallies at the ceremonies, with a good number lingering to augment the ranks of popular militants in the city. Indeed, these recruits seemed keen to surpass their new Parisian comrades in fresh zeal to smite the enemies of the Revolution at home and abroad.

With the weight of these delegations behind them, two imperatives began to reach critical mass, the first being the need for a total mobilization of the loyal French population in order to defeat the multi-sided threats to the Republic; the second, corollary to the first, entailed heightened vigilance against internal enemies when more and more able-bodied patriots had been called to the front. A "law of suspects" would authorize a widened net to detain, try, and possibly execute far greater numbers of perceived counter-revolutionaries at an accelerated pace. With the new currency of that proposal arrived the fateful phrase, "make terror the order of the day," never a formally adopted policy but more an emergent rhetorical consensus, as the only adequate resolution in the face of the pressing dangers.

As a direct consequence, the previously unhurried retribution against the Girondins gathered speed and force. At the beginning of

September, there was a renewed assault by the *sans-culottes* on the Convention, its range of demands including more severe measures against suspects. Heightened fear of traitors reinforced desperation among the sections over the supply and price of bread, reinvigorating the cause for which the unfortunate Roux had been pilloried. On 5 September, a massive march on the Convention assembled the ranks of the Paris Commune with the sectional militants, augmented by the Revolutionary Republican Women. When the marchers entered the hall, the spectator galleries erupted in applause, joined by Montagnard deputies below. The insurgents then occupied the largely empty right-hand portion of the seats, where the Girondins had once sat; some even broke into the heretofore inviolate chamber of the Committee of Public Safety to press their case. Once again, the Mountain found its options limited by popular insurgency, this time a collective embodiment of Marat's most incendiary polemics.

Prosecution of an even larger Girondin cohort began in earnest at the beginning of October, complicity in Marat's murder now among the charges. At the midpoint of that month, David made public his *Marat at His Last Breath*. Its public unveiling on 16 October suggests around six weeks of working time, an even more impressively brief interval considering David's simultaneous appointment to the busy Committee of General Security, through which the cases against the Girondins will have proceeded. On that day, David's own Section du Muséum, men, women, and children, marched in procession to honor both Marat and Lepeletier, their busts carried through the streets, accompanied by musicians, soldiers, some deputies, and fraternizing sympathizers from other popular societies (though the ceremony's falling in the middle of the working week would have held down the numbers). The march concluded in the large courtyard of the Louvre, placing the assembly close to the artist's main studio and recalling the semi-annual Salon exhibitions of painting and sculpture held in the Salon Carré of the palace. Aesthetic expectation would moreover have been heightened by the long-delayed but fervently acclaimed opening of the Louvre as a national museum, first mooted under the Old Regime but now invested with patriotic pride. Works heretofore sequestered in aristocratic palaces and royal depots made for something of a splendid, permanent Salon, its public inauguration having formed part of David's grand festival of National Unity on 10 August.

Viewing habits and expectations, it is safe to say, will have been enhanced. For this later occasion, two honorific sarcophagi had been installed in this outdoor Cour Carré, above which David's martyr portraits invited the admiration and edification of the public—at least for a few hours and from a considerable distance for most. This also happened to be the same day as Marie-Antionette's execution, an instance of simultaneity typically noted as an uncanny coincidence. But the question need be posed: just how coincidental could it have been that the public unveiling of the painting and Marie-Antoinette's arriving at the guillotine took place on the same day in October? Few in the country would have been more acutely aware than David of the former queen's finally coming face to face with judicial reckoning for her undeniable complicity with the enemies of a Revolutionary France.[19] David's specific charge at the Committee of General Security was oversight of interrogations. Though records of his movements are scarce, he is recorded as participating, alongside the Commune's fierce prosecutors Antoine-Quentin Fouquier-Tinville and Pierre-Gaspard Chaumette, in the grilling at the Temple prison on 8 October of the former princess Marie-Thérèse over the sordid, suborned testimony of sexual abuse against Marie-Antoinette by her surviving son, Louis Charles.[20] The trial date before the Revolutionary Tribunal, only six days ahead, must have been at the forefront of the artist's mind. Beginning on Monday, 14 October, the court's deliberations extended into the early hours of the 16th, thereby guaranteeing that, by morning, Marie-Antoinette

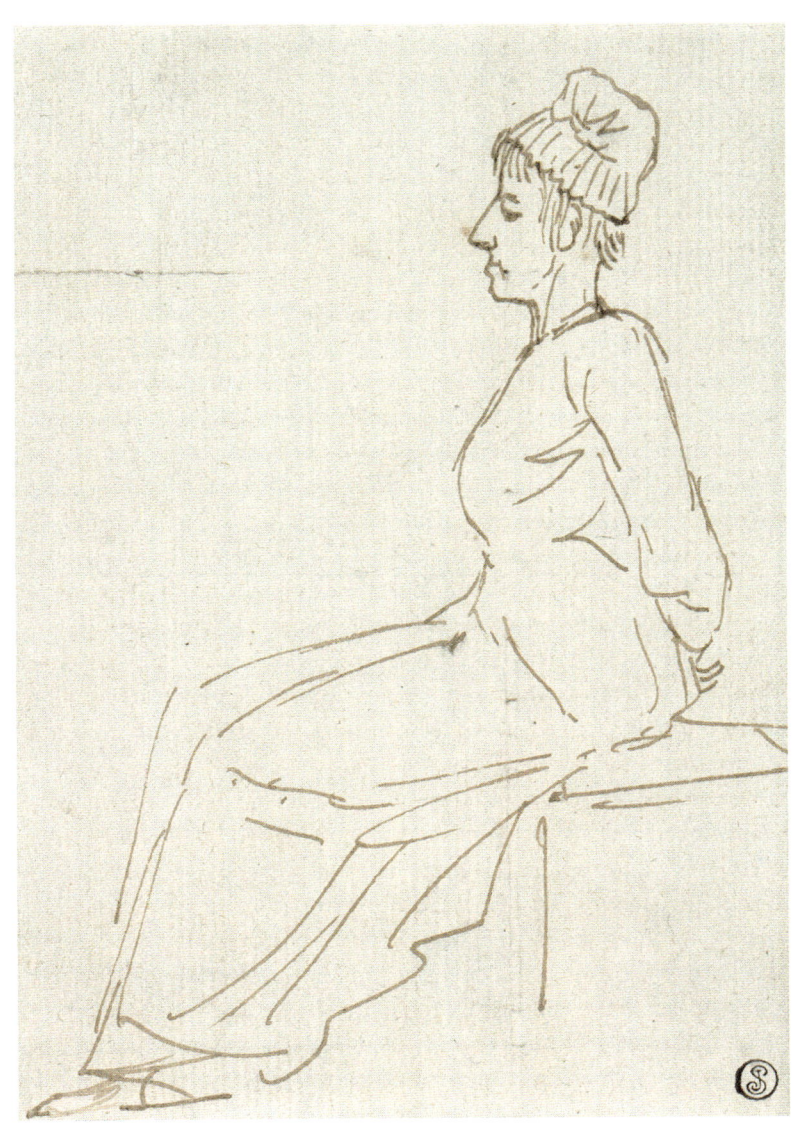

Jacques-Louis David, *Marie-Antoinette on Her Way to Her Execution*, 1793,
ink on paper, 30.5 × 42.2 cm, Paris, Musée du Louvre

would be transported by cart from the Conciergerie prison on the Ile de la Cité, down the Right Bank past the Louvre, to her place of execution in the place de la Révolution (today's place de la Concorde). The famous sketch of the humbled but upright former queen on the day has been perennially attributed to David, if lately questioned because of supposed technical and logistical impediments to its realization [*previous page*].[21] Legend identifies a certain house in the Rue Saint-Honoré as his vantage point, but David could have taken advantage of any number of slow-downs and halts along the way, including a stop in front of the Jacobin Club itself.[22] Massive crowds and organized eruptions of vituperation all imposed delays. As long as one understands his artist's impression as having been based on both glimpses in the moment and long oversight of her harrowing, weeks-long judicial disgrace, then the traditionally attested authorship can reasonably stand.

The trials of the former queen and of Marat's assassin aligned themselves with one another in the eyes of those directly responsible for both. The prosecutor of the Revolutionary Tribunal, Fouquier-Tinville, asked for the documents from Corday's examination before proceeding against Marie-Antoinette, that misogynistic template from the trial of a patent counter-revolutionary setting up the next, more inferential case.[23] The same might be said of David's sketch, as reduction of the once-glittering royal consort to the stiff, grimly tight-lipped *condamnée* parallels the symbolic splitting to which the artist had subjected Corday when he extracted her best features and lent them to Marat. Humanizing the "hideous insect" left a harridan behind as the implied remnant of the operation, to which David's drawing of the former queen lent eloquent form—as much Corday's portrait as it is the fallen monarch's.

As will emerge in the chapters to follow, David's painting invites the spectator to process an array of carefully rendered clues to her crime, just as the prosecutors of both women had made a fetish out of forensic exactitude in reaching their predetermined verdicts. At the same time, that memorial aimed to steer the thoughts of the spectator away from the martyr's dangerous former guise, the "drinker of blood," the reputed architect of the prison massacres of September 1792. But that diversion could go only so far. The next strand of David's *Marat at His Last Breath*, which provides the visual rubric for the following chapter, tracks its muted but decisive trail of blood.

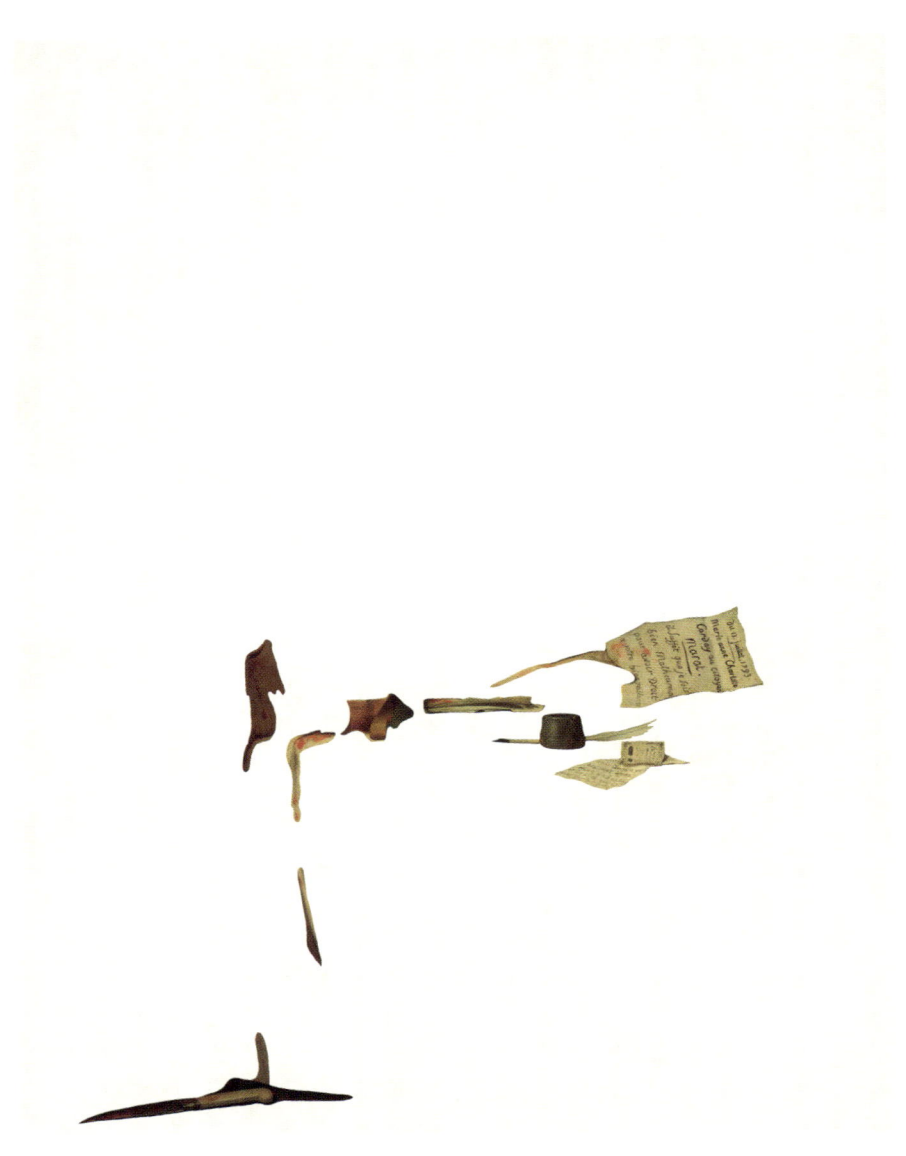

Jacques-Louis David, *Marat at His Last Breath*, 1793, image manipulation
by Dominika Ivanická, 2023

4

CIRCULATION

THERE IS NO ESCAPING A GRUESOME START to the present chapter. The medical faculties of Paris being within shouting distance of Marat's apartment, the forensic details of Corday's murderous act were observed in the minutes afterward, first by the local surgeon-dentist and subsequently by Jean Pelletan, chief physician to the Republican armies. Both were soon met there by Jacques-Philibert Guellard, the police commissioner of Marat's local section, along with its military guard. "The thrust of the knife delivered to the said Marat," Guellard attested, "penetrated under the clavicle on the right side, between the first and second rib, so deeply that the entire length of the index finger could penetrate into the wounded lung. According to the position of the organs, it is possible that the trunk of the carotid artery had been severed, which further indicated the loss of blood that had caused the death, which poured in floods from the wound."[1] In the instant of Corday's *coup de couteau*, the small room where Marat soaked and worked would have been awash in arterial blood splashed over the assassin and every surface in the vicinity—the linens, his papers and improvised desk, the floorboards. By the time these officials arrived, its flow had spread to the adjacent antechamber.

In his invaluable study, *Le Bain de l'histoire*, Guillaume Mazeau describes unanimity among the witnesses at the inquest on 16 July, as they dwelt on the red bathwater and the heaving waves ("gros bouil-lons") of blood overflowing from Marat's chest. Their "tableaux de mots" omitted none of the panicked reactions: Simone Evrard's rush to stanch the bleeding, the assistant Laurent Bas's picking up a chair to strike Corday's head and knock her to the floor, forcing the knife from her hand, Evrard's then turning, with help from the concierge, to seize the assassin by the hair.[2] But the self-possession of the Marat household turned what might have been prelude to a vengeful lynching by the crowd arriving at the door into an orderly hand-over of Corday to the guard unit of the section and its commissioner Guellard.

The moment of the victim's last breath, therefore, presented a confused picture to an artist wishing to memorialize that passage from life to death. So it merits asking why he might have insisted on such precision. The phrase may have been commonplace, but its use was conspicuous in a document that could not have been more adjacent to his undertaking. During her interrogation at the scene of the crime, Corday was found in possession of a lengthy, self-justifying "Address to the French People" (she bore it concealed at her breast, next to where the knife had been). Had she succeeded in her initial plan to kill Marat in the public concourse of the Palais Royal or at the Convention itself, she imagined herself delivering that speech over the body. "I want," the text proclaimed, "my last breath to be a service to my fellow citizens, that my head carried through Paris be a rallying symbol for all friends of our laws, that the tottering Mountain see its fall written in my blood, that I be their last victim, and that an avenged universe declare that I had well fulfilled my human destiny."[3] Her pronouncement succinctly expresses in reverse David's brief for all of his Marat commemorations, beginning with the funeral procession and ceremony described in the previous chapter. The sight of the martyr's corpse, conveyed through the streets of the capital, was meant to shore up the anxious authority of the Mountain, besieged from all sides in the wake of their Girondin purge and so left shaky indeed in its newly exclusive perch atop the pyramid of the state. His eventual painted memorial aspired to secure the more permanent approbation of posterity for Marat's vengeful vigilance where the enemies of the people were concerned.

Corday's aspiration to write her legacy in blood, however, prompted inevitable parallels—but greater pictorial problems, if only for reasons of decorum and legibility. Fresh blood of the kind that attended Marat's last breath possesses no form of its own. To render its substance with even a modicum of naturalism interferes with the formal clarity of everything else it touches, while at the same time repelling the prolonged engagement of the viewer. Blood also bears a macabre, off-putting resemblance to the painter's medium itself, both in its thickened liquidity and in its deposit of indelible stains. At the same time, as hardly needs pointing out, blood is ritually sacred, from pagan and Hebrew animal sacrifices to its Christian, human-to-divine transubstantiation into quantities of flowing (and staining) red wine. Countless effigies of the visibly wounded, bleeding savior preside over the altars before which believers consume their communion grape.

In an uncanny way, a comparable relic of Marat's rapid bleeding-out survives and, what is more, captures an instantaneous impression of the martyr's moment of death. Deemed authentic both by historical provenance and recent DNA analysis, the pages of two past issues of *L'Ami du Peuple* that he was annotating just before Corday's arrival in his room (no. 506 and no. 678, published on 30 June 1791 and 13 August 1792) were saturated by his blood. It would appear from the symmetry of the pattern that the bound pages were closed and the abundant blood soaked through the bundle [*page 68*]. Perhaps he closed the pages at Corday's approach. The dates of the two issues suggest a retrospective frame of mind where the perfidy of the royal couple was concerned: the earlier of the two having

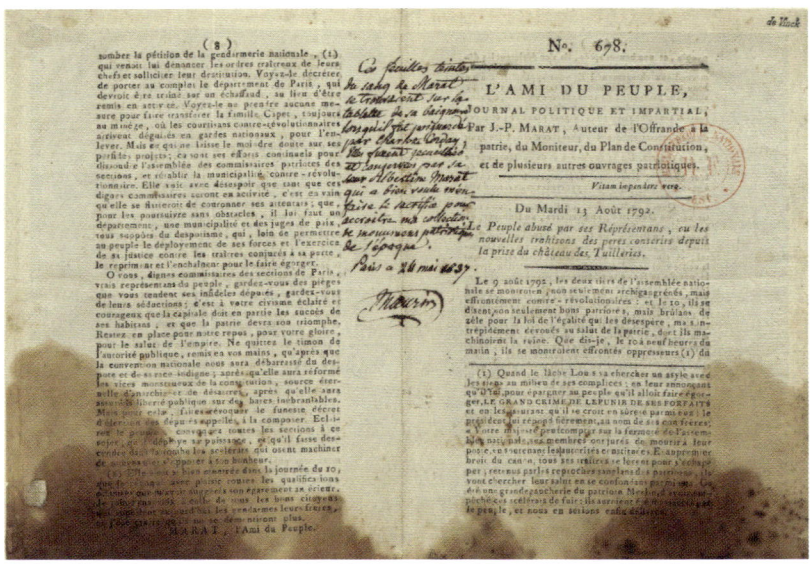

Jean-Paul Marat, ed., *L'Ami du Peuple* (13 August 1792), pages stained with blood on 13 July 1793. De Vinck collection, Cabinet des estampes, Bibliothèque nationale, Paris

been published in the aftermath of the infamous Flight to Varennes, when the king and queen had attempted to flee the country and join the powers arrayed against France; the later one dated just after the insurrection of 10 August that ended the monarchy. Rather than the police, Marat's intimates somehow saved the sheets amid the melee, and they passed into the hands of his sister, Charlotte Albertine. She, in turn, ceded them in 1837 to the autograph collector and ex-officer François-Nicolas Maurin, "to augment his collection of patriotic monuments of the epoch," as he wrote on the opening, from which they passed via another collector to the French National Library in 1909, where they lay dormant for a century.[4]

Was David aware of this astonishing survival? The sheaf of papers he depicts under Marat's left forearm would approximate the size, configuration, and placement of the old pages, as would the tinge of blood along one or two of them. That touch hardly approximates the extent of the soaked-in blood evident in the actual counterpart—but nowhere, as noted above, does David come close to reproducing the actual volume of blood that would have been present. Tracing the sanguinary pattern across the canvas of *Marat at His Last Breath* thus proves a more subtle and tenuous exercise than the previous two heuristic manipulations of the scene. Via the deft excisions by Dominika Ivanická, David's parsimonious, constellated patches of actual red pigment plot a flowing pattern all on their own [*page 64*], one that invites close attention to the shifts in meaning as one's focus moves from one trace to the next. But before undertaking that exercise, it seems imperative to address the overcharged, not to say overwhelming significance of blood in the imagination of the Revolution. The epithet of blood drinker indelibly attached to Marat arose not from anything to do with the legendary Terror, which commenced only in the months after Marat's death. It stemmed, rather, from events of the previous year that precipitated the downfall of the monarchy and provoked within days the first large-scale outbreak of murderous popular violence against the perceived enemies of the new Republic. Thus the logical sequence of our subsidiary images derived from David's *Marat* here necessitates a chronological step back.

•

Over much of the previous year, the war policy advanced by the Girondins (or Brissotins, as they were initially known, after the name of their perceived leader, the journalist and deputy J.-P. Brissot) had been met with dismaying reverses at the hands of the enemy Austrians and Prussians along the northern and eastern frontiers.

The Prussian commander, the duke of Brunswick, issued a manifesto late in 1792 warning the people of Paris, above all the "patriots" of the Assembly, of dire retribution should the royal family be molested: the invaders would "exact an exemplary and ever-memorable vengeance by delivering the city of Paris to military punishment and total destruction." The French right-wing press, still active and on the case, had been publishing lists of those to be executed when enemy troops reached the city, accompanied, in the words of the historian Peter McPhee, by "lurid images of the Seine choked with Jacobins and streets red with the blood of *sans-culottes*."⁵

While Brunswick heartily endorsed this prospect, the vengeful threats issued primarily from the French aristocratic émigrés gathered in Coblenz around the two brothers of the king, a court in exile hovering at the border ready to swoop into Paris in the train of the foreign armies. The unsuccessful effort on the part of the royal couple to join them—the infamously aborted Flight to Varennes one year before—had already discredited the king's protestations of loyalty to the new constitutional order; for most militants, the Brunswick Manifesto put their worst suspicions of treachery beyond doubt. It was at this point that the forty-eight local sections of the city formed themselves into the "Insurrectionary Commune," which came to supplant the existing departmental government of the city.⁶

On 10 August 1792, the combined force of *sans-culottes*, coordinated by the Commune, overawed the royal family in the Tuileries Palace, driving Louis XVI, Marie-Antoinette, and their two children to seek protection inside the Assembly itself. A large, finely finished drawing by François Gérard depicts them crowded and confined in the reporters' cage by the speakers' rostrum [*facing page*]. The needless provocation and tragedy of that moment, however, came afterwards, as the mercenary Swiss Guards and volunteers pledged to anyway, leaving some three hundred of them dead. Multiplying this

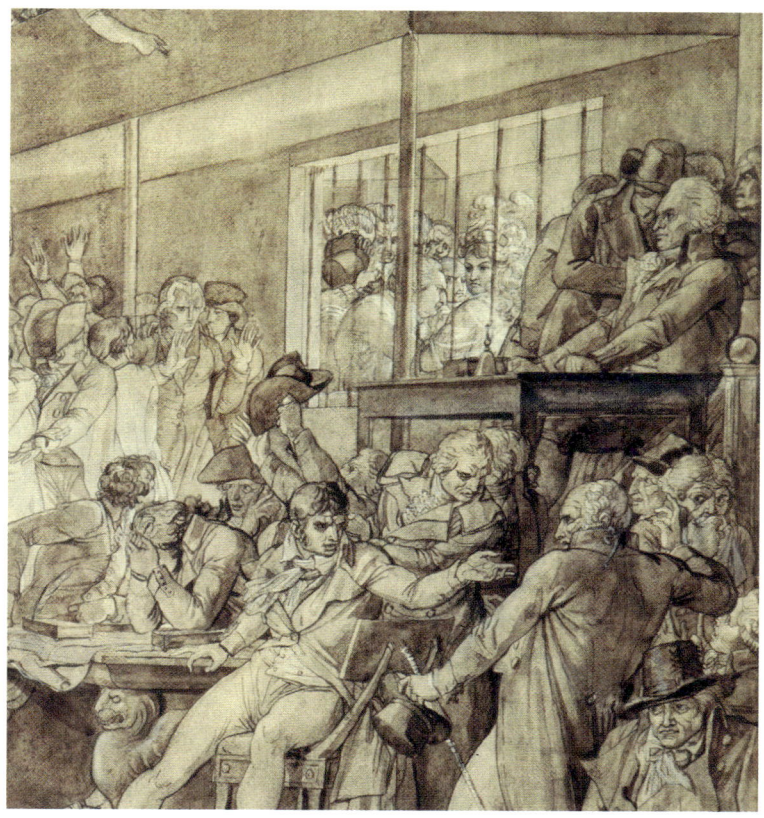

François Gérard, *10 August 1792*, 1794, ink and wash on paper,
Paris, Musée du Louvre (detail)

gratuitous massacre, Louis XVI had fecklessly released his defend-
ers from their orders. As many fled across the Tuileries Gardens,
most were cut down by enraged militants gathered there earlier as a
reserve force. This "second revolution," the birth of the First Republic, had arrived already bathed in massive quantities of fresh blood.

The Legislative Assembly, wedded to the constitutional monarchy enshrined in the first constitution, had been rendered almost moot, obliged to share authority with the new Commune as triumphant exponent of spontaneous direct democracy.

That municipal body provided the vehicle for empowering Robespierre, Marat, and David alike. The first of these, whose name virtually equates to the coming, most radical phase of the Revolution, had been a deputy to the Estates General and served in the successor National Assembly until its dissolution in September 1791 (giving way to the Legislative Assembly stipulated under the first, royalist constitution). For nearly a year since, Robespierre's only platforms had been the Jacobin club and his nearby local *section des Piques*, where he raised a lonely voice against the unpredictable hazards of the Brissotins' war policy. As those warnings proved prescient, he had instantly embraced the 10 August insurrection and successfully put himself forward for election to the Commune's Council. That renewed standing and prestige in turn propelled him to the new, national Convention charged with establishing a fully Republican legal order. An electoral body in each administrative department was empaneled to select the new deputies, with Robespierre, popular for his anti-war stance, the first chosen for Paris. Thereafter in a presiding role, he lent his endorsement to "the man who, in order to combat Lafayette and the court, had to keep himself hidden in cellars for a year," meaning Marat, who duly became the fourth deputy selected.[7] David, already a regular in the Incorruptible's tight social circle, was selected twentieth to join them in the delegation representing the capital.[8]

It testifies to the bureaucratic efficiency of the new order that the complex national apparatus for electing deputies to the new Convention had come together in a matter of weeks after the 10 August insurrection put an effective end to the monarchy. Marat's selection raised him from the outlaw fringe to a representative position of legal respectability (in response to which he changed the name of his newspaper from *Friend of the People* to *Journal of the French Republic*). Events commencing only a few days before, however, had brought back to the public mind all of his pitiless calls for violent retribution against those he had identified as the people's enemies. Despite his non-participation by express word or deed, the paroxysm of blood-soaked, improvised justice carried out in the prisons of Paris—known forever after as the September Massacres—would permanently imbue his reputation.

•

During the summer of 1792, as military reverses mounted, so did rumors of clandestine spies, saboteurs, refractory priests, and aristocrats amassing hidden caches of weapons, kin to Cataline's conspirators ripped from the pages of Cicero. The leading body within the new Commune was its Council of Surveillance, and sweeps of suspects swelled the population of all the erstwhile palaces, convents, and hospitals lately commandeered to serve as prisons. Certain incarcerated common criminals, currency forgers and black marketeers, carried a similar stigma. The aftermath of 10 August then added new numbers of arrested royalists, including the commanders of the Swiss Guard. As more and more able-bodied patriots enlisted for duty at the war front, fears grew that the prison concentrations of enemy agents and sympathizers were poised to unleash themselves on the unprotected citizens of Paris, should the foreign forces reach the city.

As major frontier defenses continued to fall, there seemed no remaining obstacle to that dire eventuality. When news reached the capital on 2 September that the key fortress of Verdun had surrendered, accumulated tension exploded. A group of *sans-culottes* fell on a cartload of prisoners being transferred to the former abbey of Saint-Germain. Once inside, they improvised a rough tribunal before which prisoners were brought one by one to plead their innocence. Some succeeded and were fraternally embraced; the majority, however, found themselves dispatched to the courtyard and summary execution by a gang wielding clubs, knives, and swords. The pattern then spread like a wave over three days across the prisons of the city, with some 1,200 prisoners brutally killed before it was over.

There was reason to believe that the executions had been condoned if not exactly organized from within the Commune, where both Robespierre and Marat were ensconced. While some Brissotin voices endorsed them as an unavoidable exigency, the horror of the episode catalyzed the fatal animosity that arose between their faction and the Mountain, it being reliably rumored that arrest warrants had been issued by the Commune for leading Brissotins (the "faction of the Gironde," as Robespierre now called them). The charge was complicity with the royal court, which would have put them directly in the way of the vigilantes. These tacit death sentences, it was said, had been quashed only by the intervention of the Jacobin deputy and minister of justice, Georges Danton. Their most grievous blame fell on the outsider Marat, whose writings had long targeted the group around Brissot as traitorous royalists in disguise. Shaking off the challenge from the Commune, the Brisssotins/Girondins had quickly consolidated a dominant position in the Convention and its ministries, buoyed by the unexpected French victory at Valmy in mid-September, which momentarily checked the foreign threat. As the previous panic eased, guilt over the excesses of the prison massacres made them seem irredeemable atrocities, with Girondins in particular keen to deflect their own responsibility. In their counter-invectives, Marat indelibly became their author, reveling in murderous mayhem and promising worse—in short, the "drinker of blood" as long as he lived.[9]

This *buveur de sang* went so far as threatening to shed blood inside the Convention itself—though the blood was his own. That moment arrived in the autumn of 1792, within weeks of his assuming his place as deputy to the Convention. Wasting little time, his Girondin enemies prepared articles of indictment and expulsion from office over a multitude of transgressions, their leading orator, Pierre-Victurnien Vergniaud, excoriating Marat as "repulsive in calumny, bile, and blood . . . who has raised his audacious head above the laws."[10] In response, Marat coolly took the rostrum for the first time in his legislative career, defying his accusers: "This furor is unworthy of free men; but I fear nothing under the sun," he protested, whereupon, as the reporter for the *Moniteur* interjects, "He draws a pistol from his pocket which he presses to his forehead," proclaiming, "I declare that if the decree of accusation is made against me, then I shall blow my brains out (*me brûlais la cervelle*) at the foot of this tribune."[11] While Marat's histrionics found little approbation, his dramatic defiance stopped the Girondin assault in its tracks, and the Convention passed on to regular business.

Henceforth, Marat would take full possession of his elected office, turning himself into one of the Convention's more prominent and distinctive orators. The slow fall of the Girondin faction over the summer of 1793, detailed in the previous chapter, seemed to have removed the threats to his well-being until Corday appeared on the scene. But the respect she was subsequently accorded in many quarters took as read the imagined Marat, soaked in gore—yet another reason for David to proceed with extreme care where his representation of the martyr's spilled blood was concerned, lest his rendering seem tacitly to endorse a narrative of justified retribution. To say that the inclusion of blood is sparing is to understate how little of it is actually on view. A few hesitant drips aside, blood explicitly exists in the painting by virtue of the things it has delicately touched and marked. But in another respect its implicit presence verges on the pervasive.

•

It would make sense to begin with the wound, the overt breach in the body's envelope. As is the case throughout, the bleeding is little in evidence. The sagging incision, outcome of a plunge with a flat blade, assumes a modified crescent shape that verges on the graceful. David emphasized its depth with dark carmine color, but the most recent seepage is gentle, slowed to a drop that echoes the shape of the wound. But perhaps it is not the latest, as just along on the sheet draping the lip of the bath is a splash of brighter red, a flung portion seeming still in flight, explainable only as a spurt having arced over the intervening flesh. Could it stand for the final exertion of a pumping heart?

The disproportionally small wound does not, however, exhaust the motif. Within its zone of the composition, the shape proliferates in roughly parallel sequence. Most proximate is the right clavicle, which is much larger, but the darkened declivity above the bone conspicuously rhymes with the shape and disposition of the wound. Following the track upward leads to the major motif of Marat's mouth, seeming to exhibit the often-imagined smile of the martyr. To return to the comparison between David's ink drawing of the head in death and its final painted rendering (noted in the previous chapter), the original downturn of the mouth—likewise evident in Mme Tussaud's death mask—has been flipped so as to answer the orientation of the wound. That the change generates an apparently peaceful, even beatific expression would have been welcome to the artist's political allies in the autumn weeks during which David brought the painting to its finished state.

This proved to be the moment when formal political executions in Paris decisively advanced from the once-and-for-all assumptions attending the king's death sentence in mid-January, to the dam's breaking, as Maizeau argues, with the execution of Corday on 17 July.[12] Not only did the ascendant Mountain find in Marat's assassination retroactive justification for the proscription of the Girondins at the start of the summer, but all the further rationale required for moving their cases on to the Revolutionary Tribunal, with the orchestrated spectacle of collective capital punishment for that faction to follow by the end of October. Corday's fate had likewise helped remove the last inhibitions against the trial and execution of the queen two weeks before. Part and parcel of this shift had been the state's effort to monopolize the violent means heretofore wielded by the popular militants, which meant a policy of subduing the rage of the crowds while substituting representative democracy for its direct manifestations. Danton had anticipated this shift in responsibility at the bar of the Convention back in March. "Let us terrify," he had famously declared, "so that the people don't have to." Even within the Convention, now on emergency "Revolutionary" footing, the majority of deputies had ceded punitive agency to the two great overseeing committees.

Nearly all of David's artistic decisions contributed to making Marat's memorial a plea for calm rather than an incitement to retribution. In the previous chapter, the artist's late decision to fill out and further close the eyelids was shown to seal the beatific transformation of the death portrait. In their consequent mirroring of the shapes of wound and mouth, these changes also disperse and dilute the already discreet character of the fatal injury, linking it by a chain of repetition to the softened, female-inflected facial features. Re-inforcing this play of correspondences among discrete motifs, intimation of blood pervades the same zone of the painting via the ruddy hue that David gave to his underpainting—that is, the darker tonal layer over which he laid mostly lighter pigments compounded from oxides of lead and antimony. This permitted him to leave visible the inherently carnal suggestion of the layer beneath to serve as shading and shadow. One place where this device crosses over to a nearly overt sanguinary signifier lies in the vertical declivity in the linens descending from Marat's visible ear, with its carmine suggestion of seepage and terminal depletion. But the same general tonality more subtly encompasses this entire portion of the canvas, from the stained bathwater to the furrowed forehead.

Marat's face and torso testify to one level of truth; the rest of the painting to another. Blood in the former, retained in subcutaneous capillaries, speaks to the fullness and continuity of life, cruelly breached and on the verge of disintegration, but for the moment maintaining its integrity. The truth to which blood attests elsewhere belongs to a different order of knowledge. It marks a discontinuous inventory of objects implicated in the crime, traces of blood being the evidence that links the one to the next. The red stain on the folded papers beneath the extended left arm launches a horizontal vector toward the letter from Corday somehow still lifted and gripped, smudged all along its lower edge with bloody fingerprints. Its only counterpart in intimacy with the malefactor beckons from the lower left of the canvas, where the fallen murder weapon lies with darker, congealing blood heaped along its blade, the smudges along the handle analogous to those on the letter above.

These manifestations of veristic evidence, nonetheless, depend on multiple deceptions and implausibilities guaranteed only by David's consummate still-life technique.[13] Where the knife is concerned, the most patent departure from reality lies in the handle of ivory, when it was actually black. Corday had purchased the kitchen implement early that day in a Palais Royal shop, sheathed in cardboard, which she carried tucked away at her breast. That alteration might seem a simple matter of artistic license, lending the implement sufficient visibility to register against the dark floorboards and allowing the incriminating traces of blood to stand out against a lighter background. As the blade already amply bears this evidence, however, why would the more sinister ebony handle not have sufficed?

While there were likely multiple reasons for David's decision, one answer lies in the letter from Corday that Marat improbably still grips. The change in the knife handle makes for an express correspondence with the lower portion of the ivory-colored paper. In keeping with the multiple equations that the painting makes between the assassin and her prey, the residues of Corday's hold on the knife align themselves with those presumably left by Marat on the notepaper. Thus they signal to one another as counterparts across the expanse of the painting's lower half. But the comparative truth-value of the two items one-sidedly favors the knife, despite its altered hue. The letter invites falsification on the grounds that Marat never saw it, Corday having written it as a sentimental alternative to the one she actually pressed on him (which promised names of traitors). Its presence further poses the question as to how these indistinct traces of blood came to be the sole residues on a sheet of paper directly in line with the spurting wound—and how Marat could have been fingering anything at that traumatic moment. Other adjustments led to the positioning of the martyr's extended thumb to emphasize the word *benevolence* in Corday's missive—the more transcendent word substituted by David for *protection*, as she had originally written.

The letter's heading, moreover, allowed David to inscribe Corday prominently into the scene via her full given names, Marie-Anne Charlotte (she was known to intimates as Marie), and do so via the action of the same hand that had held the murder weapon. That full notation of her legal name suggests the heading of a court document, a matter of pressing interest to the artist during the weeks in which he would have been making these changes to his painting. It is always worth noting how much else David had on his plate during the three months he had to complete it. Looming over him at the outset was the Festival of Unity to be enacted on 10 August, the first anniversary of the monarchy's downfall, the most elaborated and grandiose he would ever oversee. A crowd drawn from all over France was to process across most of the city between stations marked by monumental temporary sculptures, such as the colossal Egyptian goddess in the place de la Bastille, spouting regenerating water from her mammoth breasts, or the Hercules at the Invalides, the size of a tall house, representing the might of the united people trampling underfoot the hydra of Federalism. In advance of those staggering logistics was the scheduled vote to abolish all the Old Regime academies, an initiative in which David had been central as leader of the anti-royalist Commune des Arts. Then came his September appointment to the key Committee of General Security and oversight of the interrogations that preceded the referral of high-profile suspects to the Revolutionary Tribunal. That responsibility would have lent him new eyes for the forensic value of items placed in evidence at trial—and the painting renders its inventory of incriminating items as such.

Why, one might wonder, would further proof be needed regarding a criminal suspect caught in the act by multiple witnesses (among them Simone Evrard's sister, along with Marat's publishing assistant Laurent Bas who subdued Corday). Scores of onlookers had immediately gathered, with the section's security chief Guellard on the scene almost immediately to take statements. Neither had Corday at any point disputed her guilt nor withheld information sought from her. Guillaume Mazeau points out that her prosecution, nonetheless, adhered to the longstanding commitment of French jurisprudence to assembling an edifice of documentary proof. He notes that, irrespective of the preordained outcomes, "The personnel of these institutions of exception showed themselves particularly vigilant with respect to legal rights."[14] One motive behind this legalistic rigor lay in the hope that further layers of conspiracy would thereby reveal themselves. But such care became something of an end in itself, an ethos that David took on board when he assumed his investigative duties on the Police Committee, as the Committee of General Security was generally known.

Every one of the material items in David's painting functions as implicit testimony bearing on the crime and its perpetrator, high points marked in blood for investigators to follow. Corday's disingenuous letter finds its counterpoint of sincerity in the letter that Marat had putatively been in the act of writing, one addressed to a war widow, a "mother of five children." In a tour-de-force of illusionism, David extends the sheet toward the viewer so as to break the notional plane of the picture. In a modern trial, that document would likely come into play during the penalty phase, serving as the prosecution's evidence of a blameless victim; likewise, the piece of paper currency on top of it, the *assignat* that Marat had set aside for this unfortunate, patriotic family. Its markings and insignia, albeit sketchily suggested, stand in for the state itself, the Republic that guarantees the value of the note—and ultimately the disputable authority of the painting itself, whose author is its office-holding representative.

In light of David's service on the Police Committee, then, how much greater would have been his attention to the forensic dimension of his painting, in which uncommon weight rests on the rendering of script illegible to viewers even a short distance away—a fact he acknowledges in the approximate rendering of the *assignat* and the vague script in the letter to the war widow, unnecessary precision giving way to visual suggestion. In his previous painted tribute to Michel Lepeletier, he had suspended in the air an unreal specimen of writing (the martyr's vote for the death of the "tyrant") pierced by the Damoclean sword. Its counterparts in the *Marat*, by contrast, all possess some claim to have been deposited in the actual flux of events, as much as does the murder weapon itself. Allowed a close approach to the finished canvas, the viewer assumes the place of the sleuth, following David's artfully contrived clues, arranged along the incriminating trail of blood.

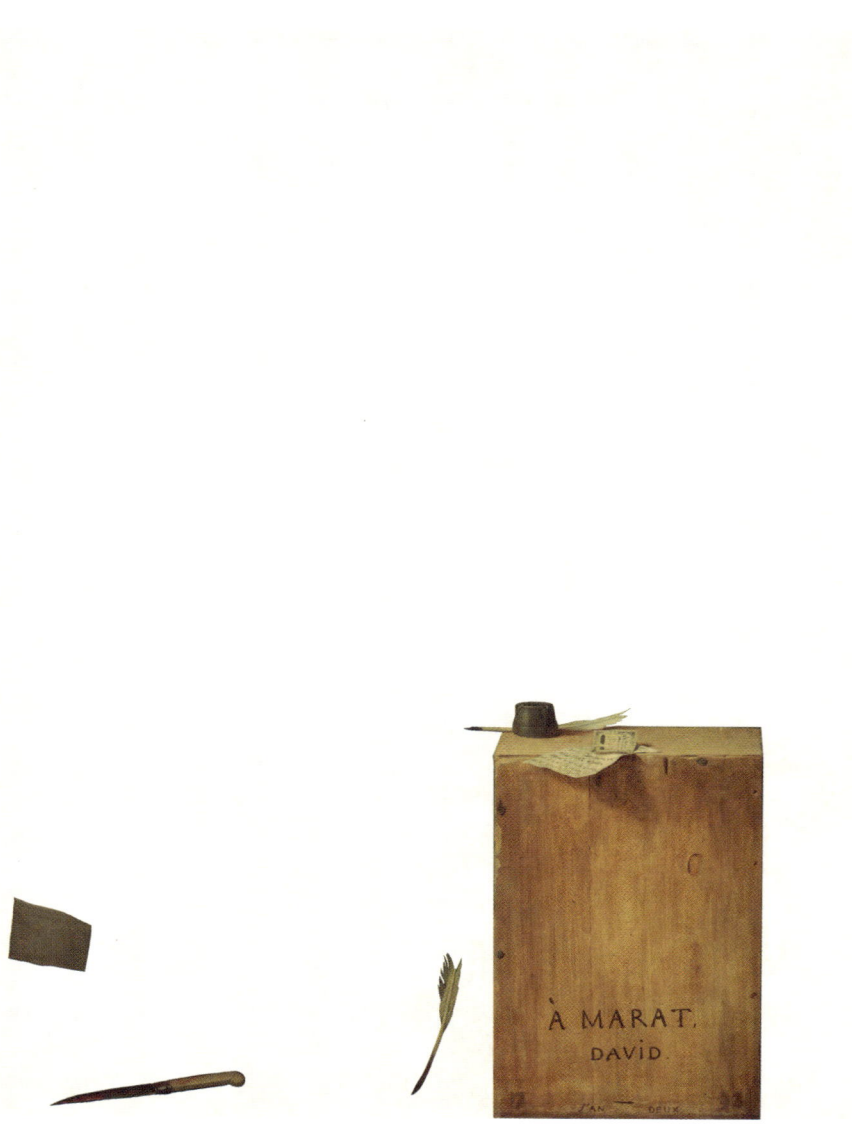

Jacques-Louis David, *Marat at His Last Breath*, 1793, image manipulation
by Dominika Ivanická, 2023

5

DEFINITION

TO EXTEND THE FORENSIC DIRECTION of the previous chapter: David invests the props and furnishings of Marat's *salle de bain* with an impressively true-to-life appearance, the Latinate word being verisimilitude (simulating truth) [*facing page*]. He was very good at that, excelling in ways that went against the grain of the hierarchy of value inculcated by the Royal Academy of Painting and Sculpture. Detailed naturalism in the depiction of ordinary objects, the province of dedicated still life, defied the decorous generalization of thought appropriate to elevated narrative subjects. To maintain internal consistency in representations of heroic action, accessories tended toward the unobtrusive, serviceable but not calling attention to themselves. No artist's way with a bronze shield or clay ewer was meant to stand out for its special virtuosity. If exemplary deeds were to maintain universal significance, too much locally contingent detail would break the spell of the ideal.

In David's rise to dominance in the pre-Revolutionary decade, he upended many conventional expectations, including this one. His 1789 *Lictors Returning to Brutus the Bodies of His Sons* has figured above for its lessons to his pupil Girodet in the representation of grief, as well as for the ways in which the painting condenses the tragedy into two figures of opposed gender and social station immobilized at opposite ends of the composition. It seems a grand

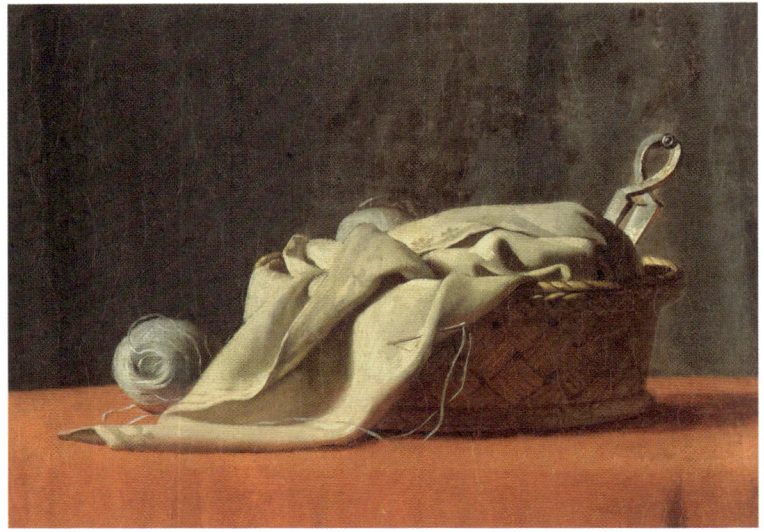

Jacques-Louis David, *The Lictors Bringing to Brutus the Bodies of His Sons*, 1789, oil on canvas, Paris, Musée du Louvre (detail)

history painting without a center, an additional defiance of academic expectations. But David had a trick up his sleeve: he placed at the center of the entire narrative apparatus the epitome of an unassuming domestic object. As the mother and sisters of the victims react (stiffly) to the overwhelming sight of the dead bodies of sons and brothers, a sewing basket with balls of thread, a needle, and archaeologically accurate shears rest abandoned on the red-draped tabletop [*above*]. The painterly care lavished with great delicacy on this ostensibly casual accessory, combined with its highlighted place at the center of events, suggests some symptomatic substitution is taking place for something that cannot be shown.

In an oil sketch, David had, in fact, tried out showing the severed head of one son being brandished on a pike above the returning

procession, but had suppressed that eye-catchingly gruesome dis-
traction from the stilled sublimity of grief below. Indeed, such a
violation of the Aristotelian dictum that actual violence or blood
had no place in tragedy would have given pause to even so bold an
innovator. But what could not be explicitly displayed could, however, be figured indirectly by the disarmingly inanimate—if executed
with sufficient eloquence. The potentially over-obvious likening
to a severed head of the ball of thread, along with the basket as a
body and the scissors as a sword, needed the tempering of a technical command to rival the great still-life specialist Chardin. Yet that
allegorical correspondence remains in play, as do the connotations
of refined needlework as the expected preoccupation of aristocratic
women. David's still-life exercise marks the necessarily unseen violence of the executions, along with the gulf in social class between
the central female group and the far more movingly grief-stricken
nurse to the far right—reversing the guiding assumption of tragic
drama, whether on stage or canvas, that the emotions of the high-
born exceed in magnitude and exemplary importance those of
simple commoners.

Roland Barthes, neglected here since the introductory chapter,
had much to say concerning the observation of naturalistic detail in
the "classical" fiction of the nineteenth century. In this visual analogy, he would have taken seriously the paradox of David's sewing
basket—the insignificant becoming central—in so far as it affirms
and ramifies reversal as the deep dynamic of the *Brutus*. He would
nonetheless have been impatient with its evocation of a proverbial
commonplace, as in: "Such are the idle pursuits of women in royal
households." These devices in fiction belong for him to the least con-
sequential of its codes, their purpose being to render "natural" all the
hidden artifice on which the efficiency of the form depends. Indeed,
on both occasions when he brings up such codes of banal reference,
he does so under the rubric of nausea: "The referential codes have a

kind of emetic virtue," he pronounces at one point, "they bring on nausea by the boredom, conformism, and disgust with repetition that establishes them."[1] Their accumulated effect of commonplace clutter, he states further, "becomes a nauseating mixture of common opinions, a smothering layer of received ideas," and, at their worst, "a fatal condition."[2]

It does no harm to entertain these strictures on artistic appeals to what he calls "the army of stereotypes," regarding them as inevitable in any naturalist idiom but essentially sub-artistic, only barely redeemable by authorial irony. But irony in David's *Marat* is scarce. Following Barthes in this regard relegates certain recurrent issues in the work's interpretation to secondary importance. There is no escape, for example, from the patent correspondence between the bloody knife and the quill pen still held in the fallen hand. But as soon as one thinks of the formula "The pen is mightier than the sword" (as antiquated in French as it is in English), any sense of discernment entailed in that recognition collapses into humdrum cliché.

Much the same can be said of the hammered-together wooden crate that served as Marat's writing stand [*facing page*]. By David's own description of the room from his visit on 12 July, that object ought to be a cylindrical, sawn-off log or chopping block (*billot de bois*). By transforming the motif into one of rectilinear geometry, reinforced by the uncannily naturalistic woodgrain, the analogy to the base of the cross is secured. The artist's inscription, À MARAT, / DAVID, hovering between an applied signature and an actual property of the wooden surface, replaces with fraternal affirmation the mocking INRI (Jesus of Nazareth King of the Jews) in the scriptural account. Despite all the back-and-forth arguments as to how Christological David's martyr portrait might be, none of these features rises above the inherent banality that Barthes assigns to every such prosaic cultural reference: all leave to one side whatever it might be that constitutes the superlative character of the work to which

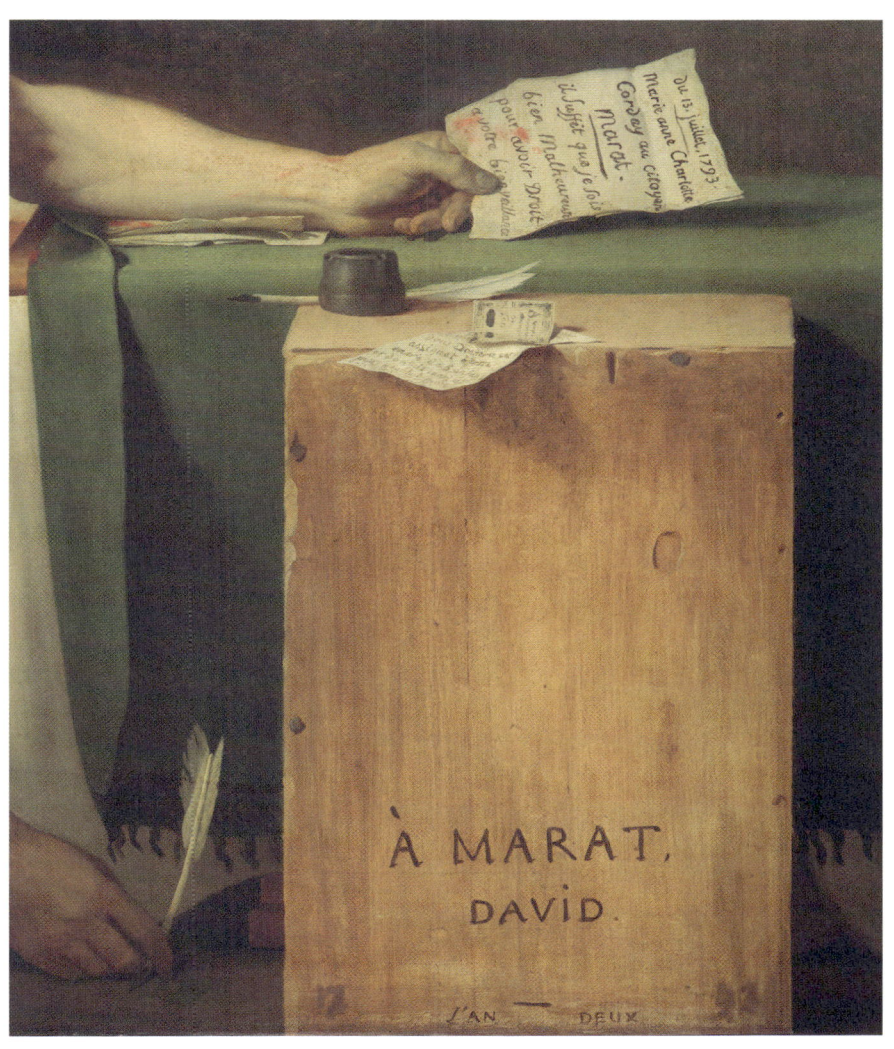

Jacques-Louis David, *Marat at His Last Breath*, 1793, oil on canvas,
Brussels, Royal Museums of Belgium (detail)

intuition so persuasively testifies. Nor does the accumulation of such references somehow raise the whole to a level above their individual inadequacy, none more so than the imperfectly effaced numerals 17 and 93, half-heartedly replaced by the date L'AN DEUX from the new Revolutionary calendar—which had yet to be adopted at the time of the murder.

In a painting of this caliber, however, no motif can be exhausted by its correlation to this or that entry in a standard cultural dictionary. Other relationships and correspondences orchestrated inside the picture operate in ways that escape being so routinely conventionalized. The dying Marat's headwrap can signal the character's infirmity and ill health but becomes other to itself once transposed into the work's inner dynamic of gender interpenetration and fusion [*page 40*]. The blood-laden knife participates in another network of traces that follow—as seen in the previous chapter—a forensic, evidentiary itinerary designed to exercise the mind rather than lull it into complacency [*page 64*]. The plain wooden crate, so easily enlisted as a stand-in for stele or cross, turns out to pose even more cerebral conundra bearing on the truth value of pictorial data—and thus, by indirect implication, the veracity of Marat as witness, prophet, and worthy object of mourning.

•

How high would the crate be? About a meter? Anachronistic, to be sure, in that the metric system had yet to be adopted: *pieds* and *pouces* would have been the current units of measurement. But that is the scale. Beyond its duties as furniture, the box serves to position the viewer's implied eye level. That turns out to be just above the object's top edge, so that Marat's writing surface presents itself at a steep, receding angle. Fully apprehending this detail places one's gaze well below the center axis of the format, when alignment with the roughly horizontal axis of the martyr's head would have been expected. While such may still be the case, that implied viewpoint obtains only for that zone of the composition occupied by the figure. Inconsistencies in perspective are not surprising in the portrait genre, as other forms of harmony can readily outweigh spatial rigor. But *Marat at His Last Breath* offers an overall sense of calculated, rectilinear proportion that promises exactitude in all its parts. And David further encourages this expectation by positioning the crate in such a way that the notional lower edge of the box does not just meet the actual edge of the wooden stretcher beneath; the two boundaries become so close as to be one and the same. Thus the ground plane is stopped in its implied projection forward into the space being occupied by the viewer—which is a good thing, too. With the floor construed as parallel to the writing surface, a consistent viewing angle would require an eye at too great a distance even to see all that the painting contains. Conversely, answering the invitation to savor that detail on the righthand side implies a closer viewing position, virtually down on one's knees, despite the fact that such a vantage point would entail looking up at Marat's distorted facial features from below. Rebecca Comay speaks of spectators' necks being uncomfortably twisted by coordinating perceptions of the painting in its various parts.[3]

Like the "red wheelbarrow" of William Carlos Williams, so much depends upon the front of the crate coinciding exactly with the transparent fourth wall of the painted scene. David reinforces that effect by breaking that boundary with Marat's charitable letter precariously extending over the forward edge of its top, while casting a shadow on its all-important face. Just as important in this regard is the strict parallelism between the right vertical margin of the painting and its echo in the nearest vertical edge of the crate. To achieve this, David has played once again with the implied viewer's position, such that one would need to be positioned far to the right in order to see the edges of the crate's front and top align to form one continuous straight line (if ever so slightly bent near the top). The interval between box and border forms an almost abstract rectangle of commensurable regularity, faintly naturalized by the tassels at the border of the green baize cloth.

On the opposite side of the crate, by contrast, the top edge slants away at an angle, and the natural disorder and entropy of the world take over: the jutting corner is coming apart, as irregular knocks, dents, and conspicuous nail heads assert themselves below. That worn, blunted, upper corner testifies to rough use, as do the heavier nail heads that contrast with the vanishingly small holes regularly spaced down the opposite side. The bigger nails would have been banged in later as a repair, with lateral stresses then widening the openings in the soft wood around them, all of these details testifying to David's extraordinary way with still life. While a continuation of his contrarian attitude toward academic hierarchies, the rendering of these details plays its part in the specific mission of this particular painting. Owing to the immense emotional and political investment the relatively modest canvas was obliged to carry, with its primary subject half-obscured and off to one side, the necessary eloquence of the work needed to be distributed across every depicted feature— even, as will soon emerge, passages that seem to have no features at all. In service to this imperative, the wooden crate provides the necessary counterweight to the likewise de-centered figure of the martyr himself, the two entities balanced at either end of the diagonal, upper-left to lower-right axis around which the painting is organized: the barely living Marat at one pole, the honorific inscription of his name at the other. Like heavy, orbiting stars, the two dominant entities warp the space around them, their two incommensurable zones tempered by more subtle symmetries and correspondences.

The crate further acquires a certain speaking capacity as conveyed by the martyr's words projecting forward from its top into the viewer's space. In the world David creates for the body of his friend, those written words stand for the truth of its subject's self-sacrificing commitment to the cause of the common people, such that the implied volume of the wooden container becomes a whole substitute for the incomplete body of its speaking subject. The quill pen and inkpot stand behind as the tragically muted organs of truthful testimony, while the crate provides more than a convenient platform for such anthropomorphic analogies. It presents its own test of veracity, which begins with David's implicitly asking if this thing is indeed what we think we see: a regular, hollow, geometric volume composed of no less than three larger rectangular sides and either one or two smaller, square ends.

But how does an alert viewer reach that conclusion on the basis of the parsimonious visual evidence presented? Only one surface presents itself in anything like its full measure, that of the inscribed boards that align themselves so seamlessly with the implied picture surface. David is careful to position the crate so that the adjacent two sides are invisible and unknowable to viewers answering the invitation to scrutinize the motif with care. To go about inferring the truth of the whole from points and angles would engage the Cartesian core of the French philosophical tradition. Geometry offers a touchstone of veracity in visual representation, as its theorems are subject to demonstration and proof independently of any material embodiment of the entities concerned. David's eccentric, that is, ex-centric positioning of the viewer's gaze onto the emphatically regular, upright volume invites geometric inference, but, at the same time, undermines its exercise by so emphasizing the distressed material substance of the two visible surfaces.

The geometrician may posit planes and angles but generally does not saw and hammer them into place. The emphatic outline of the crate finds a subtle, but far from insignificant echo directly to its left in the rectangular, neatly hemmed patch on the sheet that drapes the bath [*page 92*]. As another sign of both the frugality of the poor

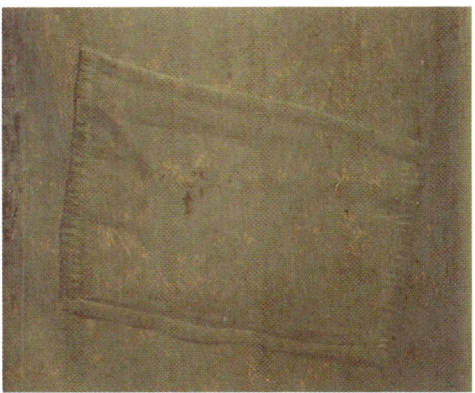

Jacques-Louis David, *Marat at His Last Breath*, 1793,
oil on canvas, Brussels, Royal Museums of Belgium
(detail)

and the domestic virtue of the Marat household, it hardly rises above allegorical cliché. But it could be construed as a more specific surrogate for Simone Evrard, the loyal, virtuous antithesis of Charlotte Corday, thus entering the higher gender economy of the painting, then finding a place within its regime of geometry by constituting an object analogous to the discrete entities elsewhere in the painting. In a topological sense, this caringly rendered detail maintains its continuity as rectangle whatever the contingent distortions of its material substrate—just as does the letter paper projecting from the crate's top, which corresponds in apparent size to the cloth patch and synthesizes the evocation of virtuous womanhood with a perceptual puzzle of foreshortened shape.

To see it as illustrated above demands more in the way of viewing gymnastics, settling into a crouch or deeply bending over. Such an attentive viewer is thus encouraged to compare just how these rival truths, presented at equivalent intensity, might coincide or diverge.

Is it possible to state what the crate would be if bestowed with full being in the world?[4] There is no indication that David has truncated the frame such that the crate might continue out of view below; a faint shadow all along the lower margin even suggests a slight inward beveling to the edge, but with no indication of an end panel meeting the floor that would echo the closing piece on the upper end, the one supporting the papers, ink, and pen. David lavishes attention on the latter, using a liquid flourish of light ochre paint to trace the upper-left corner in such a way that the apparently worn-down panel in front reveals the shadowed edge of the one at the top—just at the point, moreover, where the *trompe-l'oeil* letter crosses the boundary. In a pile-up of resonant motifs above are suspended the black inkpot and the curled fingers of Marat's left hand.

David's consummate technique rewards reorienting one's gaze directly in line with the crate and lingering long enough to puzzle over all these eloquent details, along with the deceptively simple application of dilute medium ochre over light underpainting which captures the grain of the wood without resorting to over-meticulous rendering. But the vividness of that presence only emphasizes the degree to which perception of the object in the round must follow from contemplation of what is in effect a single rectangular plane. That the artist withholds so many salient clues preserves a certain enigma about the object analogous to the conundra engineered into the truncated figure of his Marat: male or female? robust or moribund? transfigured or mundane? saint or fiend? alive or dead?

To recruit the battered crate into, say, an allegory of Marat's support among the militant market women—who, after all, first dragged the king and queen back to Paris from Versailles in 1789—would be in keeping with the larger message of the painting. But such an inference would again demote what is an insistently heightened presence to the status of received common knowledge. Possibly more germane would be the use of these personal objects (or their surrogates) in the ceremonies staged in Marat's honor, which is to say, their transformation into relics. Seven weeks after the murder, when the club of Republican Revolutionary Women inaugurated a wooden obelisk memorializing the martyr, four of the *citoyennes* carried on their shoulders the bathtub in which Marat had been killed, while four more carried his chair, table, pen, and paper, respectively—or so it was said; the *billot de bois* must have been heavy for one person to bear.[5] David's enumeration of the last four objects perform a relic-like function, as their apparent wholeness and clarity of description balance and stand in for the soft, incomplete presence of the sacrificed body.

Such reverential treatment promotes the banal to the otherworldly. But is there a position in between? More than a century later, phenomenologists in the discipline of philosophy would classify the enhanced, isolating vividness invested in the objects around Marat under the technical term *eidetic*. Arriving at such concentrated awareness of this or any object, they would argue, requires setting to one side [bracketing] all culturally derived associations, with the aim of clarifying the spontaneous intuition of such "intentional" entities—all consciousness necessarily being consciousness *of* something.[6] That David so restricts the knowability of this example only enhances that effect. Similar intensity of description falls equally on non-eidetic—that is, accidental features like the cracks and knothole—such that the viewer is enlisted in the task of seeing through such naturalistic contingencies to reach the defining essentials of the object with its sacred overtones. The exercise thus imposes conditions of uncertainty and self-examination congruent with the paradoxes that attended Marat as a public figure.

The extent of Barthes's impatience with the sub-aesthetic furnishings of naturalistic fiction follows in part from the limitations of language as compared to the capacities of visual representation. Not that the latter precludes an abundance of perfunctory filler, but there is, nonetheless, the capacity, in the right hands, to endow a sewing basket or a wooden box with a presence of such eloquence that would require multiple paragraphs of prose description to approximate—and then at the cost of awkward blocks of inert exposition standing in the way of narrative progression. The novels of his contemporary Alain Robbe-Grillet incorporate relentless fixation on surfaces, but do so as an exceptional, avant-garde project. Despite Barthes's believing himself to have superseded Jean-Paul Sartre's solipsistic subjectivity, the protagonist of *Nausea*, Sartre's best-known early novel, evinces a disgust with the oppressive presence of non-sentient things that anticipates Barthes. In an apposite moment in the narrative, its protagonist, Roquentin, tunes out the conversation of a needy bore he had charitably invited to lunch. Suddenly aware of the dessert knife in his hand, he is overcome by its oppressive contingency: "My hand holds it. My hand. . . . what good is it to be always touching something? Objects are not made to be touched. It is better to slip between them, avoiding them as much as possible. Sometimes you take one of them in your hand and you have to drop it quickly. The knife falls on the plate." The mimetic visual arts, preeminently painting, could hardly be exempt from something of the same choking surfeit of gross matter ("I'm suffocating," despairs Roquentin on fleeing the café, "Existence penetrates me everywhere, through the eyes, the nose, the mouth."[7]). If one can slip through it, however, what lies on the other side? For all of David's great ability to transfigure still-life objects toward complex meanings, his *Marat* itself turns away from its crowded foreground to seek relief in an equal and opposite void.

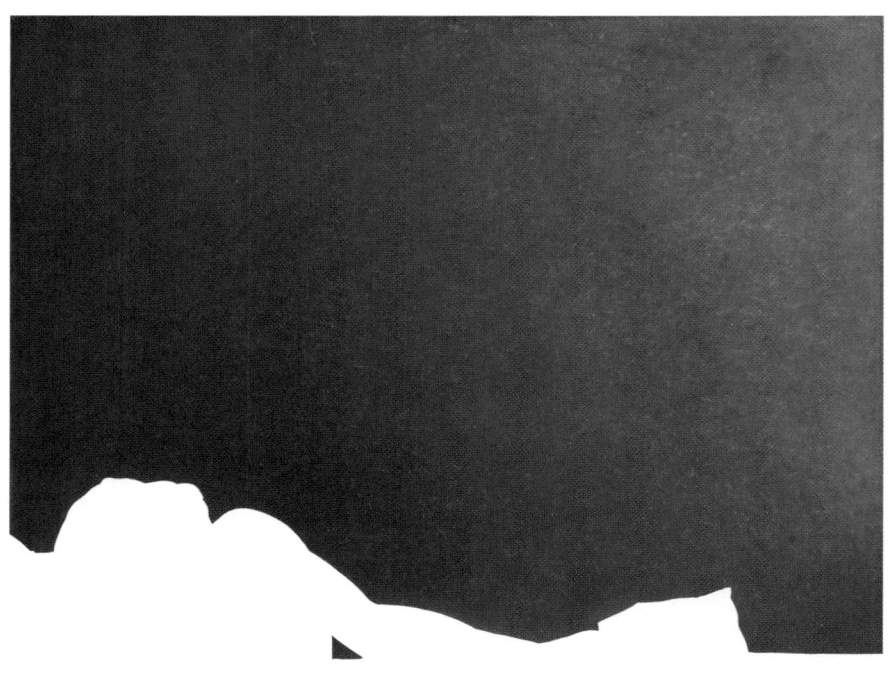

Jacques-Louis David, *Marat at His Last Breath*, 1793, image manipulation by Dominika Ivanická, 2023

6

BEYOND DEFINITION

THE NAME OF JEAN-PAUL SARTRE makes its appearance just at
the end of the previous chapter as an almost inevitable point of reference. *Being and Nothingness*, his foundational philosophical treatise
of 1943, could have provided a joint title for that chapter and this
one together. Indeed, the wooden crate in David's *Marat* precisely
exemplifies Sartre's theory of the "region of being" to which the first
term refers. But "nothingness," as it turns out, signifies for Sartre
not its opposite or absence, but another, complementary "region
of being" taken in its largest sense. Sartre's text thus belongs to the
perennial philosophical argument over whether nothing can actually
be something.

The region of David's painting isolated in the illustration on the facing page might be said to offer a similarly affirmative, if mute answer
to that same question. It cannot be said that this large expanse of
painted canvas lacks substance or offers no occasion for intentional
perception, for all that it lacks definition and eludes description.
It is indistinct but exaggeratedly so, just as the objects below are
commensurably exaggerated in their eidetic distinctiveness. In this
one respect, they are unified, but all the more to underscore their
extreme unlikeness. The crate would belong to Sartre's category of
being-in-itself—everything that merely takes up space in the world,
which includes those oppressively impinging objects instanced at

the close of the last chapter. The background of the *Marat* might conversely lay claim to Sartre's other mode of being, the "for-itself," which for him has no prescribed form and can be said to exist exclusively by virtue of human consciousness and choice. David's field of repetitive, translucent, non-mimetic touches of paint would indeed be nothing without the concentrated, questioning attention of its viewers.

The two categories, however, are by no means to be so neatly distinguished, as David's unfigured background would, in Sartre's conception, be already latent within the discrete objects below: "Fully positive realities . . . nonetheless retain negation as the condition of the sharpness of their contours, as that which fixes them as they are. . . . It becomes impossible to hurl these negations back into some extra-worldly nothingness, as they are conditions of reality, dispersed throughout being and supported by being."[1] There is no need to enlist Sartre as any sort of anachronistic authority to take advantage of this succinct statement of his philosophical problem:

> Although the concept of being has this peculiarity of being divided into two regions without communication, we must nevertheless explain how these two regions can be placed under the same heading. That will necessitate the investigation of these two types of being, and it is evident that we cannot grasp the true meaning of either one until we can establish their true connection with the notion of being in general and the relations that unite them.[2]

For "concept of being" in the first line, substitute "*Marat at His Last Breath*," and the key point is made: all of the many formal and technical observations about the painting's background are idle unless its traits are construed in active relation to the naturalistic paraphernalia that crowd the foreground. The excision of the foreground by Dominika Ivanická makes plain one salient fact concerning the

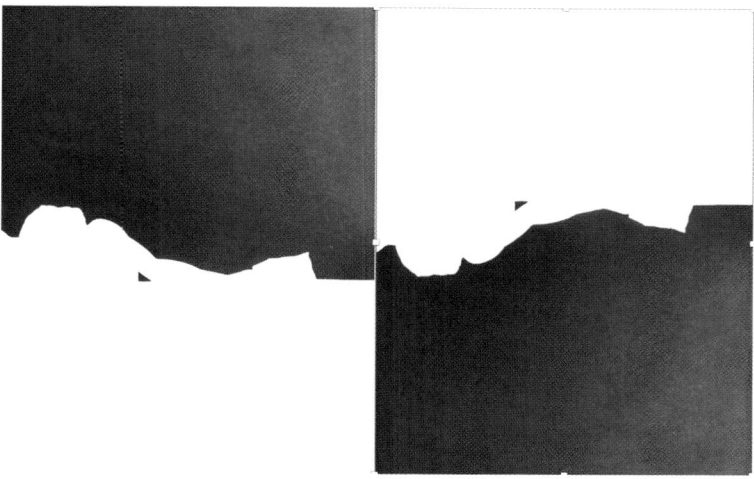

Jacques-Louis David, *Marat at His Last Breath*, 1793, image manipulation by
Dominika Ivanická, 2023, upright and vertically reversed juxtaposed

painting's two regions of being, which is that they are as closely as
possible the same size. If our altered version is flipped and placed
side-by-side with the upright version, it is even more apparent that
he had calculated their equivalence with minimal remainder [*above*].

The rock wall of the tomb in Girodet's 1790 *Pietà* has already been
cited for its parallel proportions to the upper zone of the *Marat*,
where the faint glow in its top right corner might be taken for a
reminiscence of the dawn glimpsed beyond the biblical cave (see
p. 30). If so, that prompt helped David subtly and effectively to balance the heavy, asymmetrical position of Marat's body, even in opposition to the scene's ostensible illumination from the left. Much more
importantly, however, the unusually spare upper half of his pupil's
composition would have reinforced the crucial equilibrium between
being and nothingness in the *Marat*. That is, a plethora of worldly

entities carries no more size and weight than the barely differentiated field of monochrome pigment, which functions as a discrete, aniconic figure in its own right.

But figuring how? The most recent technical analysis of the work, conducted in 2023, finds little unusual about the background, only that "the *frottis* technique consists of the juxtaposition of brushstrokes split up and oriented differently depending on the location," adding that these touches are "mainly made of iron (hydro)oxides and carbon black."[3] The French word *frottis* translates to the unappealing English word *smear*, thinned paint being applied with pressure, spreading the bristles of a blunt brush in ways that let the underpainting show through in places, in others less so or not at all. The striking luminescence of the broad, porous field arises from the underpainting being lighter than its coat of *frottis*, with the faint glow evident in the upper right achieved by slightly lessening the opacity and/or density of the dark touches. But that degree of internal variation in no way interrupts the sustained consistency of accumulated touches that constitute this demarcated half of the painted surface.

Backgrounds are by definition subordinated to the representation of the people and things in front of them. Contemporaries such as the portrait specialist Elisabeth Vigée-Lebrun had been using the *frottis* technique for a decade, but Vigée-Lebrun conformed to expectations by using such fields of indistinct marks to surround and heighten the distinctiveness of the sitter [*facing page*]. There would have been no possibility that the background be allowed its own domain, interacting with the portrait subject by mere abutment or juxtaposition. To extract a subordinate function and transform it into an eidetic object of perception on its own serves to isolate the indeterminate from the determined and reckon with its separate and equal contribution. As Sartre speaks of "being-for-itself" as "always in question . . . always in suspense because it is constantly pending," so the grand internal partition of *Marat at His Last Breath* places the future,

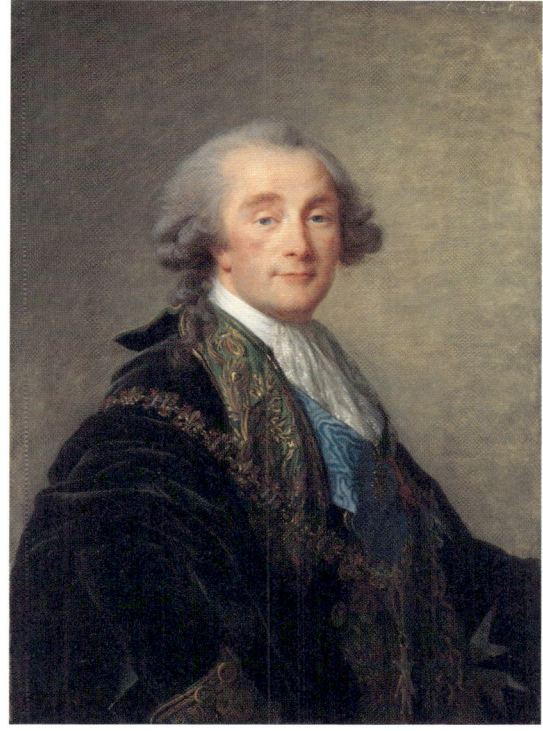

Elisabeth Vigée-Lebrun, *Charles Emmanuel de Crussol-Florensac*, 1787, oil on canvas, 89.9 × 64.8 cm, New York, The Metropolitan Museum of Art

by definition undetermined, on a par with the categorical pastness of death.[4]

David had begun recalibrating the foreground-background relation as early as 1788 in his monumental portrait of the chemist and financier Antoine Lavoisier with his artist-spouse Marie-Anne Pierette Paulze, whom David had taught and on whom he bestows pride of place over her husband [*facing page*].[5] Competing for attention, however, are the experimental implements of the chemist's epoch-making discoveries (he was first to isolate oxygen). Allegorical accessories spill from the table to the floor, albeit with luxe qualities in line with Lavoisier's vast wealth (down to the buckle on his shoe). The same can be said for the paraphernalia of writing and recording experimental results; while Marie-Anne's battered artist's portfolio, an everyday accessory for David, retreats to the shadows, no match for the extraordinary skirt that marks her fashionable rather than vocational identity. Invested with such vividness, inanimate things assert themselves at the expense of the more blandly characterized human subjects.

Five years before the *Marat*, then, David had innovated an equivalence between a background of emphatic plainness and a crowded foreground full of incident, its heightened empirical veracity in keeping with the function of the gleaming laboratory equipment in ascertaining objective truth. But he tempers the starkness of the divide with stately pilasters closing things off at the rear, which renders the difference between the *Lavoisiers* and the *Marat* one of kind rather than degree. The complete and continuous line separating the upper and lower halves in the latter is such that the "setting" of the scene lies on the further side of a horizon. It is in the nature of horizons to possess no physical reality but instead to present perpetually receding limits on what can be known. Moreover, they define space on the scale of a landscape rather than an interior, such that the distance between foreground and background in David's painting eludes estimation, with the scene exceeding the confinement of Marat's *salle de bain* to enter an unbounded realm of possibility inspired and enabled by the martyr's exemplary existence.

That expanse transforms into an observable entity what could be called, with Sartre, a zone of being "always in question . . . always in suspense because it is constantly pending." In place of dense

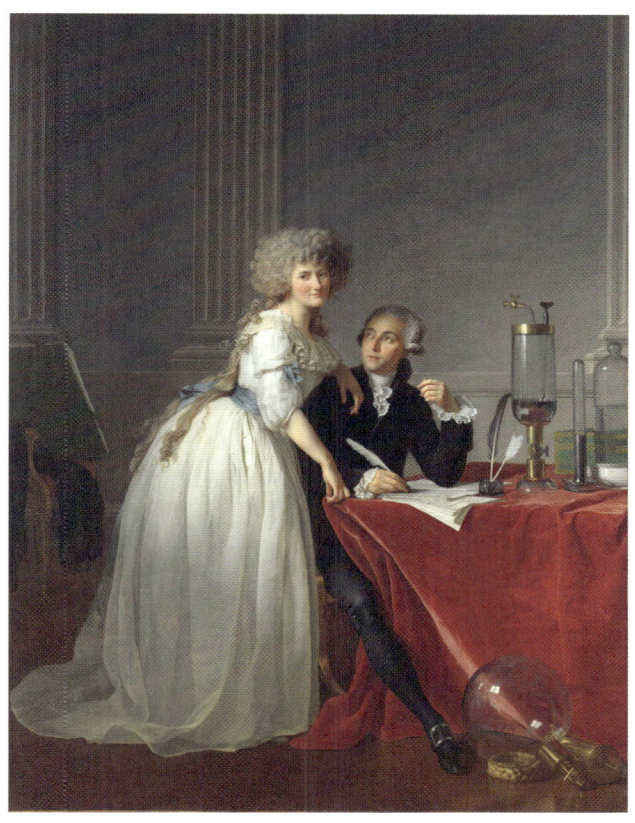

Jacques-Louis David, *Antoine Lavoisier and Marie-Anne Pierette Paulze*, 1788, oil on canvas, 259.7 × 194.6 cm, New York, The Metropolitan Museum of Art

philosophical argument spread over more than 600 pages, however, David just went ahead and painted it, projecting the particularities of Marat's example into a future yet to be formed but there to be shaped. For a philosophical generation as inclined to advance their arguments via novels or plays as in learned papers, it might not have seemed far-fetched that a painting in the right hands might somehow "do" philosophy. The question nonetheless remains as to how it could address a concept 150 years in advance of its articulation in philosophical discourse? But the evident anachronism may be less extreme than it appears. Sartre largely took his two regions of being, the in-itself and for-itself, from Hegel, whom his generation treated as a virtual contemporary.[6] The lifespans of Hegel and David substantially overlap, though this would not be for a moment to suppose that the artist entertained self-conscious ideas along these lines. But David's *Marat* elevates its honorific function less with allegorical embellishments than with a sophisticated set of propositions concerning the limits of perception, the question of time, the veracity of visual evidence, and the aims of history.

What was more, the weeks of its making coincided with a phase of exceptional contestation over the meaning of the Revolution: did it have most to do with physical things, controlling the scarce means of subsistence? Such would have been the conviction of Marat's most hardcore *sans-culotte* following. Or was there a higher priority in forging an egalitarian legal order legitimately endowed with powers over life and death? Such would have been the mission of Robespierre and a government operating, despite having promulgated a new constitution, on a provisional, emergency basis. Or would the acute uncertainties exacerbated by Corday's intervention only linger in an irresolvable amalgam of fear and hope? The preferred outcome of no one.

The philosophical points of reference adduced here arose, moreover, from historical circumstances in Paris that exacerbated risks and moral uncertainties not so dissimilar to those of 1793. So observed the philosopher Maurice Merleau-Ponty, looking back just after the conclusion of World War II: "Since 1939, we have, of course, not lived through any Marxist revolution, but we have been through a war and an occupation, the two experiences being comparable in that both involved *questioning what can be taken for granted."*[7] Sartre published *Being and Nothingness* in 1943, which is to say, under occupation and relentless surveillance by a bloodthirsty, dictatorial power. Even the formerly well-off struggled with shortages of basic foodstuffs and general privation. Though the thinkers in this circle endured as part of a subordinated population, their reflections on the imperative of politics bore striking resemblance to those of the Jacobins in their contested hegemony over the Revolutionary order. The defeat of 1940, Merleau-Ponty continues,

> had the value of a radical doubt and a revolutionary significance because it laid bare the contingency of the foundations of legal-ity and showed how one constructs a new legality. For the first time in a long while, one could witness the dissociation of formal legality and moral authority; the state apparatus lost its legiti-macy and its sacred character in favor of a state yet to be built and existing only in the will of men. For the first time in ages every officer and official, instead of living in the shadow of an established state, found himself invited to question himself on the nature of the social pact and to reconstitute the state through his choice.

With the German defeat in 1944 had arrived a new round of dilemmas, now over both the risks and temptations of violence as seen from the winning side. For left-wing intellectuals schooled in moral objections to colonial repression and violence, the postwar executions of leading collaborators divided the Algerian-born Albert Camus, who stuck to those principles, from Sartre and Simone de Beauvoir, who supported the execution of collaborators. For his part, Merleau-Ponty came to terms with the violent legacy of the French Communist Party as inherited from Stalin's prewar show trials in the Soviet Union, where hundreds of old Bolsheviks went to their deaths following forced confessions. In the 1946 tract *Humanism and Terror* (the source of the above quotations), the genial philosopher mounts an argument rationalizing that monstrous episode, predicated on the world-historical inevitability of the existing, Soviet-directed party as the sole instrument for achieving a classless society. In the special revolutionary logic he propounds, Stalin's victims become so many Girondins and Dantonists, old Revolutionaries all, put to death by the Mountain and its popular allies for similarly lofty reasons of historical necessity. Sartre and de Beauvoir joined him in adherence to the Party, the tortured logic of party lines finding some compensation in their common philosophical drive to establish fundamental conditions for truth to experience.

Such had been David's brief in 1793, its outcome open to inspection for the postwar intelligentsia in Paris. On the bicentenary of David's birth in 1948, the first modern retrospective devoted to France's preeminent artist of revolution unfurled itself across a display encompassing both Paris and Versailles. But the artist's political fortunes had followed the opposite trajectory to the one experienced by the Parisian existentialists. On his completion of *Marat at His Last Breath*, he would have less than a year free of the legal jeopardy and political disgrace that came with the fall of the Mountain on 9 Thermidor year III (27 July 1794). Circumstances were such that he made no comparably decisive artistic statement during the dwindling days left to the Revolutionary Republic. But one further call to commemorate a martyr to that Republic prompted a migration of the charged *frottis* technique to that undertaking, indeed to the virtual exclusion of all the other arrows in his technical quiver.

•

The lingering conflict with ultra-Catholic rebels in the western region of the Vendée offered up this new sacrifice in December 1793 (Frimaire year II). Bertrand Barère, the regular spokesman for the

Committee of Public Safety, in reporting to the Convention on the progress of the campaign, placed into the record a letter from one of the Republican commanders operating in the region between Cholet and Angers in the western Loire. The dispatch found space for a story of exceptional and fatal bravery on the part of a mere boy, one Joseph Bara:

> Too young to enroll in the forces of the Republic but burning to serve, this child had accompanied me throughout the last year mounted and equipped as a hussar: the whole army has been astonished to see him confront every danger, always charging at the head of the cavalry . . . This courageous child, when yesterday surrounded by brigands, chose to die rather than surrender and hand over the two horses he was leading. As virtuous as he was brave, he gave to his mother all he earned, save what he need-ed to keep himself clothed and fed; he leaves her with several daughters and his younger invalid brother, and she has no other means of support.[8]

The tale practically leaps from the letter that David had placed in the hand of his Marat, the missive to "the mother of five children," whose husband had died in combat defending the Republic in these years of perpetual conflict with internal and external enemies. Marat spares a modest paper *assignat* for the unfortunate widow; Barère asks the Convention to award a pension to the bereaved, destitute family of Bara. Approval was a forgone conclusion, the motif of the boy as his single parent's sole support having seized Robespierre's propagandistic imagination. This badge of filial virtue would be repeated automatically with every public evocation of Bara's name. At one point, Bara's mother—who happened to live in the nearby village of Palaiseau—was brought to the Convention in person, escorted by a ceremonial delegation of women from a Paris sec-tion, which is to say, the precise counterparts of those who had kept

Marat's corpse perfumed and covered with flowers. To prolonged general applause, she and her bereaved family were summoned to mount the rostrum; with a kiss from the Convention's president, she was told, "you have lost nothing, your son is not dead, he has been given a new life, the immortality for which he was born."[9] It was then left to the enthusiastic Barère to specify that this model be "traced by the brushes of the famous David" and distributed in reproduction to every primary school in the land: against the corrosions of pride and ambition found in "generals, legislators, and philosophers," he proclaimed, "Here we find absolute virtue, simple and modest, as it is delivered from the hands of Nature."[10]

The actual men of state who heard or read these words would have had reason to dread the violently paranoid drive for purity behind this seraphic image of the adolescent martyr, for which Angel of Death would not be too excessive a term. Once the shouts had died down, Robespierre was prompted to link terror to unstained virtue. Evoking the boy's having "nourished" his mother, he apostrophized, "Bara, you have already received the reward of your heroism, the Fatherland [la Patrie] has adopted your mother; the Fatherland, by choking the life from the criminal factions, will raise itself triumphantly on the ruins of vices and thrones." In that rhetorical movement, the nation assumes the inverted role of child nurturing a parent, and the child in turn becomes the nemesis of traitors. The Republic finds itself wholly embodied in a being of perfect innocence, that condition including and entailing a heedless ferocity toward its enemies ("the whole army has been astonished to see him confront every danger, always charging at the head of the cavalry"). In contrast to all the back-and-forth over whether Marat had deserved enshrining in the Pantheon or whether the Pantheon deserved him, Robespierre proclaimed the immediate necessity of Pantheonization for this new young martyr.

•

Robespierre's initial indulgence of the cult of Marat had been a negotiation between the apprehensions of the ruling committees and the symbolic needs of the Paris sections. Careful management had been necessary in simultaneously indulging the emotional attachments of the martyr's devotees and checking the prominent militants who most forcefully claimed to be speaking in his name, whether from the Commune, the sections, or the pages of the radical press. That same month the Commune had been stripped of its insurrectionary status and returned to its old functions of municipal administration. Jacques Roux was in prison and would die there by suicide within a few months. The opportunity presented by the story of Bara allowed the leader, on behalf of the Committee of Public Safety, to devise an alternative cult entirely adapted to his own purposes, such that the elaboration of story into legend coincided with a purging of the Commune early in 1794. Once a new compliant leadership had been installed, there was little danger of independent forms of ritual emerging from below. When the section bearing Marat's name attempted to revive his personal cult, the government committees responded by banning all "partial" festivals not celebrated throughout the Republic according to the plans of Robespierre and, naturally, David

Only three days before assuming personal control of Bara's commemoration, Robespierre had offered to the Convention his first extended justification of the Terror in philosophical and moral terms, a report that marked the definitive passage of organized violence from the agenda of insurgent *sans-culottes* to the integral policy of the Revolutionary government. The necessary complement to that extreme of ferocity was an equally extreme vision of uncompromised virtue: "this young child [who] nourished his mother with his pay, his cares divided equally between filial love and love of country. We could not choose a more beautiful example, a more perfect model." From David's point of view, however, such clarity would have been more elusive. How was he to move from the celebration of two mature martyrs, who were both significant historical actors and personally known to him, to the secular apotheosis of an unknown boy? How was he to ennoble what was hardly more than an unlucky act of bravado? And how was he to find non-stereotypical form for the abstract stereotypes of outraged innocence and the sacrifice of youth with which he was forced to work, following Robespierre's unreal dictum that "the French alone have thirteen-year-old heroes?" As Bara himself was now nothing but ashes, the artist had no independent experience of his subject on which to rely, seeing that Robespierre's oratorical metaphysics of purity and supernatural rebirth conjured an effigy freed from all but minimal earthly attachments in an ecstatic state even in suffering and death. Gone was the anchor of the material realm, Sartre's things-in-themselves, that had served him so well for Marat. But what remained at his disposal was the hovering non-nothingness he had fashioned for the top half of that painting, the insubstantial pure potentiality of a Revolutionary future. The key to the economy of the *Marat* had lain in its drama of stark contrast between two resplendent realms of being, but now he was effectively reduced by circumstances to one. Which is exactly how he chose to proceed, fashioning an entire battle tableau from scattered *frottis*, semi-transparent marks in a restricted palette, put to illusionistic use by varying their density and direction as if they were being roiled from within by turbulent energies [*facing page*].

This martyr would thus be a figure both of and made from the future itself.[11] Set against an expanse of nearly featureless embankment, the body floats in a cradling, almost amniotic medium of its own substance, signs of conflict only fleetingly registered at the very edge of vision to the left. The haze of scumbled mark-making necessarily condenses itself into greater concentration to establish the minimal mass of Bara's body, with paler pigments deployed on the torso and the one visible arm to bring forward the victim's physical

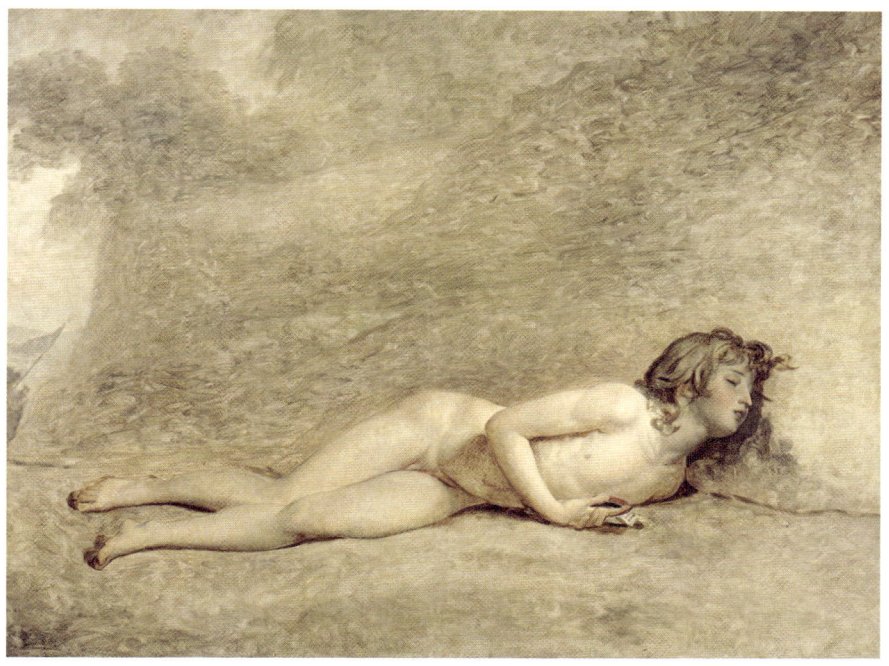

Jacques-Louis David, *The Death of Bara*, 1794, oil on canvas, 118 × 155 cm, Avignon, Musée Calvet

volume—all without breaking abruptly from the field-effect of the whole canvas. But there are certain, telling points, like the further lower leg and the flowing locks framing the facial features, when figure and setting nearly merge.

In keeping with the deep indeterminacy of Bara's persona was David's decision to forgo all contemporary costume, with the token exception of the Revolutionary cockade, the ubiquitous tricolor ornament that the boy clutches to his breast. Elimination of constraining, contingent garments, mired in the here and now, necessarily yields a state of nudity. And nudity connected the resulting figure to the deep, idealizing tradition of the ephebic male nude—"ephebe" designating the young athlete/warrior of Greek antiquity. As David would well have known, the ephebe stood for a transitory moment of maximum sexual desirability in the eyes of the older males who frequented the gymnasia where these lithe trainees prepared for the games and ultimately for battle.

That insistent connotation represented a problem in light of Robespierre's insistence on outraged innocence and a childlike devotion to his mother and country alike. Suppression of the male genitalia then became advisable, but doubly difficult in that the fatal thrust had been to the boy's midsection. As the overall illumination and blond light foreclosed the device of veiling shadow, David's response was to give the body a decidedly unnatural twist, simultaneously to figure its suffering and to downplay its gender, wrenching the upper leg behind the lower one (as the boy seems to be rolling over on to his chest, the expected position of the legs would be the reverse of this). The logic for the anomalous arrangement comes from an identifiable substitution of a direct classical analogue, as David borrows the hips and legs of the very prototype of antique androgyny, the Borghese Hermaphrodite [*facing page*]. Just as he had derived the design of the *Marat* from the contour of the Virgin in Girodet's *Pietà,* he once again abstracted and displaced a pattern of line from another work of art into his own. In this case, he traced the contour of the Hermaphrodite in its most common view from the rear rather than from the front. The entire upper contour of Bara's body, particularly the raised hip, is determined by a similar superimposition of the two-dimensional contour of the Hellenistic prototype, while the strangely effaced treatment of the genitals follows the pattern of lines created by the lower buttocks and inner thighs of the antique statue. In an attempt to impose some unity across the disjointed bodies compressed within the figure's contours, David resorted to

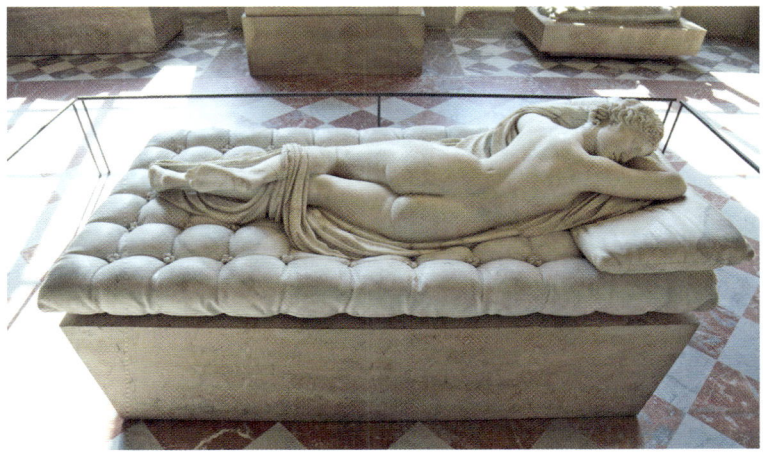

Sleeping Hermaphrodite, Roman, marble copy of 2nd century BCE Greek bronze; mattress by Gian Lorenzo Bernini, Paris, Musée du Louvre

discreet but clear markings of sexual stimulation repeated across the figure, in the trace of red paint along the crease that marks the disappearance of the genitals and its rhyme in the similar trace that follows the lower lip.

This borrowed uncertainty of sex, overlaying the representation of an unseen but mortal wound, depends upon this simultaneous transparency and reversal at the primary locus of erotic sensation, yielding the eerie ambivalence of aspect that has puzzled (and troubled) observers ever since. The more subtle androgyny with which David invested the body of Marat emerged from the artist's conflicted brief, one that entailed crafting a new, chimeric artistic genre suspended between an individual portrait and a narrative history. As the latter required more than one actor, the female antagonist parasitically occupies and thus alters what had been a single body previously perceived in terms of strident masculine ferocity. The martyr emerges from the operation suitably softened for the purposes of mourning and elegy, but not as any sort of stably intersex personage. Impressions of the painted Marat's androgyny arise as a composite effect rather than any predetermined theme that the painting was meant to illustrate; instead, any one association is perpetually replaced by another, each with differing gender valences, such that no unitary position predominates.

As extracted, not to say liberated, from the technical repertoire of the *Marat*, the formal vocabulary of the *Bara* asserts itself as nearly all flux and indeterminacy. That it condenses itself into a recognizable human figure appears almost provisional, the young boy yet so insubstantial as to float as much as fall to the ground. The borrowed outline from the Hermaphrodite functions much as did the line dividing David's *Marat* along the head and torso of the expiring martyr, condensing the notional whole of the violated body into a bare line borrowed from another, apposite work of art. Such are the clashing forces at work in the composition that the body of Bara appears nearly broken in two, awkwardly sutured together at its midsection.

David's erudition was such that Ovid's origin story of Hermaphroditus in the *Metamorphoses* could not have been absent from his thoughts. Paramount in that narrative is the fusion of two beings, one male and one female. The fabulously beautiful son of Hermes and Aphrodite, hence the name, finds himself the object of the overwhelming sexual passion of the nymph Salmacis. Surprising him as he bathes in her spring unaware, she wraps herself tightly around his body, exclaiming, "Willful boy, you can resist me, but you can't escape" and calls on the gods to make them inseparable: "Now these two figures in their close embrace were two no longer, but were something else, no longer to be called a man and woman, and although neither, nonetheless seemed both" [IV: 508–520].[12] Barthes, too, must have had this passage in mind when writing later on the subject of absence and longing: "The two sides of androgynous being sigh for each other, as though each breath, each incomplete breath, were seeking to merge with the other. Which would be the image of an embrace, for it melts the two images into one."[13]

Such recognition of fluidity along the gender spectrum, confounding determinate identities, remains largely absent in *S/Z*, interpretive tour de force though it is. So there would seem still to be unfinished business over the adequacy and the possible blind spots in the Barthean model on which this inquiry has been based, as it requires that symbolic castration be the solution to the riddle of the text: "*Beneath La Zambinella*," states Barthes categorically, "there is the *nothing* of castration." Fixated on Balzac's transvestite castrato, his analysis comes to an abrupt halt at the revelation of that "scandalous" physical state. By his own testimony, however, Barthes had been feeling some ambivalence over the frame of castration anxiety by the time that *S/Z* was published, going so far as to say that he regarded its adoption as "ludique," a playful or quotational borrowing that might pass itself along like pocket change or an even an illness. In an interview with his colleague Raymond Bellour, he entertained the idea of an alternative discourse of psychoanalysis, not a restrictive clinical ideology but rather "an accession to the infinitely permutative play of a language beyond the subject."[14]

Had he held out that prospect in the pages of *S/Z*, its staying power would have been all the greater. Two of his former students have more recently recalled that their use of the term "castration" in the seminar verged on the obsessional, as its members found in it a seemingly endless "capacity to scramble boundaries, to transgress the separation of the sexes, to engender a form of writing truly liberated from the tyranny of clear distinctions and definitions."[15] Such qualifying second thoughts perhaps tacitly acknowledge just how decisively the orthodox function of the castration complex closes down the openness achieved by the fine-grained textual analysis that precedes it.[16] And it is open to serious question whether the term "castration" could have fulfilled the role they imagined for it, when the hybrids they thought it to encompass (they instance "androgyny, hermaphroditism, transsexuality") possess their own signifiers for a reason. Granting the supposition that castration reduces gender to a nullity, hermaphrodism conversely offers gender in superabundance, with David's *Bara* manifesting along its spectrum.

Ovid's *Metamorphoses* being one of antiquity's greatest mythological repositories, the present inquiry has returned to its point of departure in the realm of myth as theorized by Claude Lévi-Strauss, Sartre's contemporary and intellectual sparring partner. Not part of their dialogue but emerging from the present discussion might be the supposition that the open-ended future entailed in being-for-itself, when untethered from the material here and now, can settle back into the well-worn channels of myth. Thus the hypothesis becomes not so much that David found a convenient template in the visual and poetic representations of Hermaphroditus, but rather that myth itself had overtaken his art, such that the distortions and oddities of his boy-martyr portrait come from a place apart from his own willful imagination. As Vincent Descombes put it in a citation given above, "The narrator of a myth is simply actualizing the possibilities inherent in the code, or in the signifying system to which he submits in order to speak. In the end, it is indeed the structure that decides what may—sometimes what must—be said on a given occasion."[17] The myths recounted by Ovid entertain virtually all the points on the non-binary spectrum, though, in keeping with the ultimately normative function of mythology, subjecting transgressors to severe exemplary punishments.

If the *Bara* participates in myth as much or more than it illustrates one, so would the *Marat* from which it emanates; so would *Sarrasine*; and so might *S/Z*. Is such a thing possible among the moderns, who are regularly credited with retrieving and reviving the mythic repertoire of antiquity, but rarely taxed with serving it involuntarily?

Barthes was eager to posit just that in the famous newspaper essays, collected under the title *Mythologies*, which he devoted to the popular culture of his own time. But nowhere in *S/Z* does he allow that his "classical" text might have eluded capture only to capture him in return. Closely cognate themes of sexual ambiguity and confusion proliferated in the literary moment to which Balzac's *Sarrasine* belongs, indeed forcefully so in other writings of his own. In an uncanny way, these outlandish tales cumulatively retrace Ovid over this same terrain. And in so doing, one finds, they likewise bear on the fundamental structuralist recognition that the human capacity for sign making comes bound inside the circuits of sexual exchange.

Might such reflections likewise bear on the status of David's *Marat* in particular? So far in the present account, derivation of its analysis from *Sarrasine* and *S/Z* might seem no more than a convenient inspiration or analogy. At the conclusion of that interpretive trajectory, however, its course raises the more subtle question as to what extent (returning to the first-person voice of chapter one) my hitting on this particular painting as an object of inquiry cognate with the Balzac story might have been driven by some actual entanglement between text and canvas. Not only does *S/Z* exert its force on the understanding of the *Marat*, but the painting, in turn, when interrogated at the same level, exerts its own, reciprocal force on the Barthesean model, exposing some of its shortcomings while pointing toward both enlargement and complication in its potential scope. My concluding chapter thus departs from the representation of Marat for an interval to pursue the further implications of Balzac's *Sarrasine* in the envisioning of transgression and revolt, both in literature and in the visual art of David's heirs.

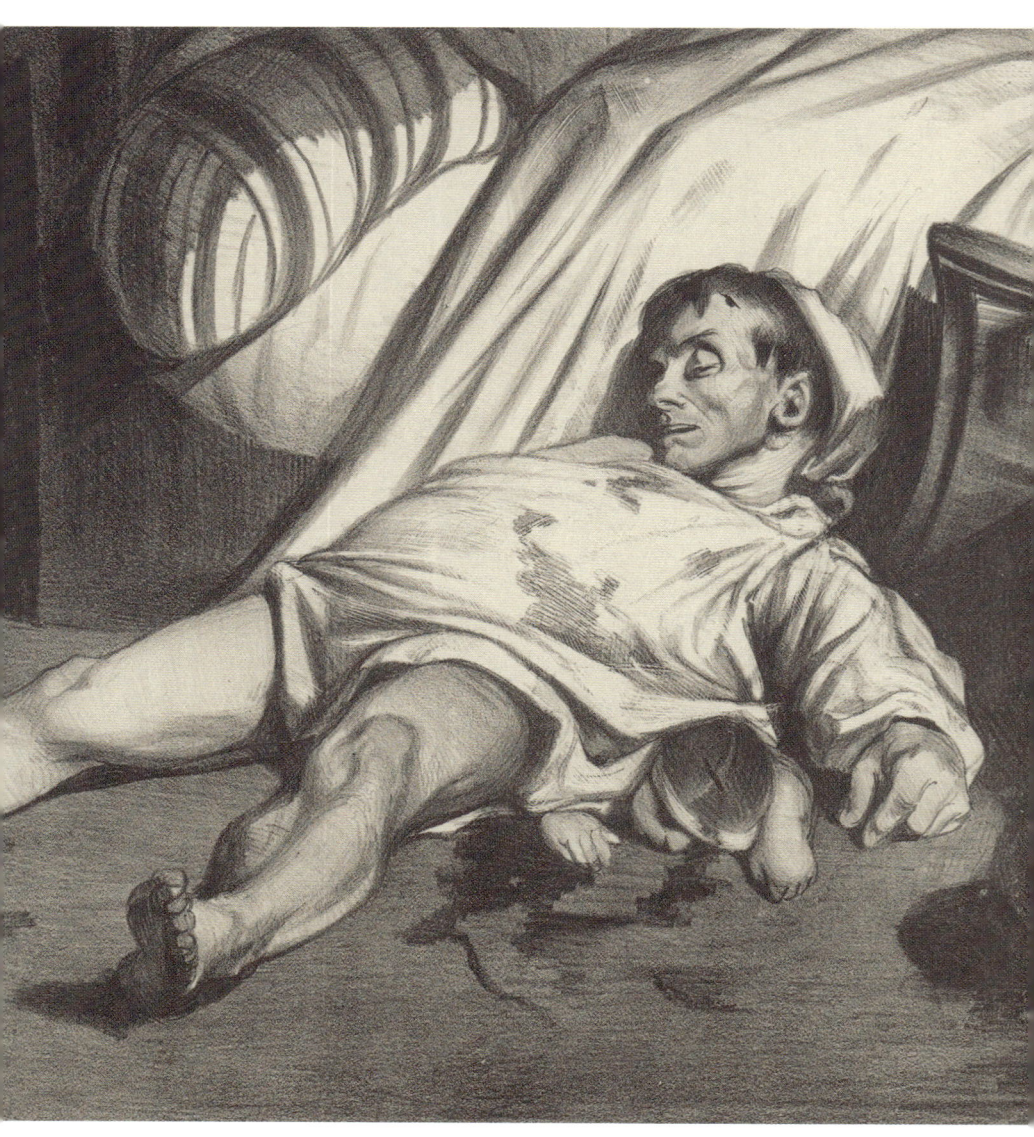

Honoré Daumier, *Rue Transnonain, le 13 avril 1834*, lithograph on paper (detail)

7

THE NEW *MARAT*

IF NOTHING ELSE, THE STRUCTURALIST moment in French intellectual history laid claim to understanding the core requirements of human signification as manifested in every sphere of activity from marriage options to plant categories to places of residence to telling of tales. Linguistic rules did not differ in kind from those governing the rest of culture's defining features, as language is both their medium and the most clarified template for social codes in general. Parallel inquiry into the analogous realms of painting and sculpture, however, lagged considerably behind. But the eighteenth century, being a period of rich speculation on the origins of social institutions, extended that curiosity to the visual arts. And already present was the connection of sign making to the alternations of erotic presence and absence.

An origin account in the *Natural History* of the Roman writer Pliny [XXXV: 151] sufficed for both drawing and sculpture, its protagonist the potter Butades of Sikyon, who lived in Corinth with his daughter, Kora. As her lover prepared to depart for a long absence abroad, she sought to remember him by outlining the shadow of his profile cast on a wall. Her father then filled in her outline with clay, modeling the face into the first sculpted portrait (from which innovation, states Pliny, he built a thriving business molding terracotta faces for the ends of roof beams). But it was not relief sculpture

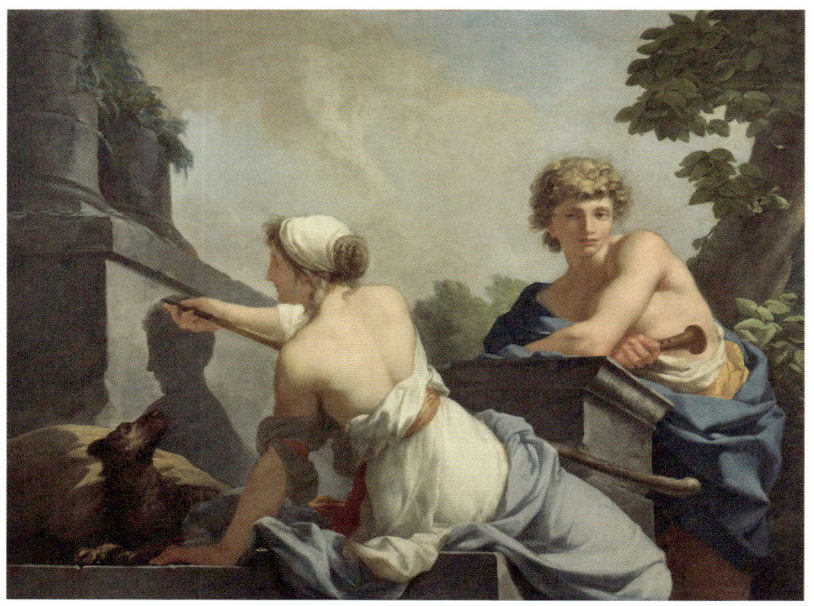

Jean-Baptiste Regnault, *The Origin of Painting*, 1785, oil on canvas, 140 × 120 cm,
Versailles, Musée National du Château

but two-dimensional art in general for which the Corinthian Maid
received the credit. Between about 1770 and 1820, which is to say,
over the transition from the *galanterie* of the late Rococo to a more
chastened Neo-Classicism, artists were regularly drawn to the tale,
as in the 1785 canvas by David's rival Jean-Baptiste Regnault. The
commission for the painting, titled the *Origin of Painting* [*above*],
had come from no less a patron than Marie-Antoinette, for whom
the artist supplied a pendant, the *Origin of Sculpture* [*facing page*].
His protagonist in the latter, however, was not the practical Butades authorized by Pliny, but rather the thoroughly mythical sculptor
Pygmalion and the female figure with which he fell in love.

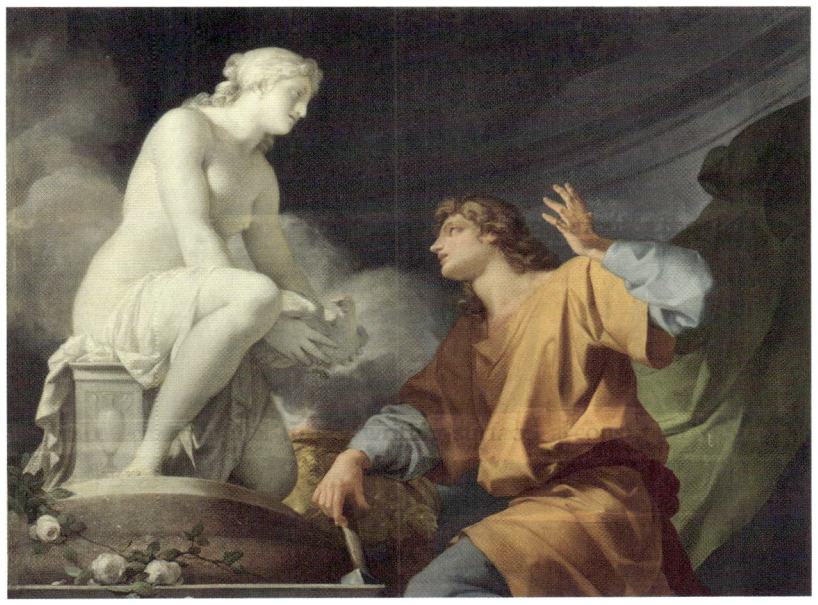

Jean-Baptiste Regnault, *The Origin of Sculpture*, 1785, oil on canvas, 140 × 120 cm,
Versailles, Musée National du Château

The parallel between the two subjects is inexact, unless one takes
Pygmalion's ivory statue to have been the first work of sculpture,
which has never really been part of the myth. The premise of Ovid's
rendition, voiced by the defeated and disillusioned Orpheus, comes
closer to the theme. The rage of Aphrodite toward certain Cyprian
sisters who scanted her worship first reduced them to prostitution,
then, "as their shame ceased, and they lost the power of blushing,
they turned to stone" [x: 307–311].[1] Witnessing their "sordid inde-
cency" had led the virtuous Pygmalion (like the narrator Orpheus)
to renounce women, turning to art for a substitute and going so far
as to caress and adorn his statue before taking her to his bed. The

goddess, having just turned living women into stone, then reversed the procedure by breathing life into dead matter and bestowing the now-living maiden on Pygmalion as his wife.

The plain implications of incest in the Pygmalion tale prove themselves out with a vengeance in Ovid, as the granddaughter of the couple, after consummating by deception her sexual passion for her father, suffers transformation into the myrrh tree. At the same time, there is symmetry in that the properly exogamous character of the Corinthian maid is equally plain, her love being for what is distant and thus, in its absence, requiring a sign; whereas Pygmalion's simulacrum of virtuous womanhood floated free of any referent, to be effaced by the unmediated presence of a living woman in a marriage of extra-human origin.

The pertinence of all this to the work at hand, however, depends upon that cycle of myth reproducing itself in the modern historical period in ways that bear directly on Barthes's undertaking in *S/Z*. Which it did. Between 1830 and 1835, Balzac produced a cycle of three stories that reconfigured the elements of this mythic pairing—Kora of Sikyon with Pygmalion—into increasingly complex structures of exchange. *Sarrasine* had come first; the second, serialized over the first two issues of the magazine *L'Artiste* in 1831, became the best known of the three as *Le Chef-d'oeuvre inconnu*, widely read in English translation as *The Unknown Masterpiece*.[2]

While the brief tale has long enjoyed renown as a powerful parable of art's unfulfilled dream of rivalling reality, comparison with the subsequently famous (owing to Barthes) *Sarrasine* helps place it firmly within this deeper lineage. Balzac sets the story in the early seventeenth century, when Nicolas Poussin, touchstone of the French academic tradition, is yet a diffident art student newly arrived in Paris. Like *Sarrasine*'s young male narrator, he encounters at the start of the narrative an enigmatically bizarre old man of mysterious wealth. In contrast to that clued-in socialite, however,

Poussin has no knowledge of this particular specter's identity, as he accidently accompanies him into the studio of the experienced artist Franz Pourbus. The other visitor, it transpires, is the legendarily reclusive master Frenhofer, who proceeds to subject a painted female figure by his host to withering critique. Rehearsing the theme of antithesis that governs the opening pages of *Sarrasine*, the master finds Pourbus's effort distressingly half alive and half dead. Seizing a palette and brushes, he adds no more than a touch here and there, but astonishes the two witnesses with the palpable life suddenly bursting from the entirety of this *Marie égyptienne*.

Poussin and Pourbus pay a return visit to Frenhofer's residence, the occasion for Balzac to indulge at length in a detailed inventory of its opulent furnishings. Off limits, however, is his inner sanctum of a studio, where for ten years he has labored over a female figure rumored to be so lifelike as to erase the distinction between the living subject and its representation. Having witnessed his preternatural skills in action, his visitors express their longing to view the miraculous portrait, at which point Balzac makes patent his parallel to Ovid's Pygmalion: "What? . . . Show my creature, my spouse," Frenhofer exclaims, "tear off the veil with which I have chastely hidden my joy? It would be prostitution. For ten years I have lived with this woman; she is mine, mine alone!"

The ending of the story, however, offers nothing like the blessing of Aphrodite. Balzac supplies Poussin with a young lover of surpassing beauty, whose tearfully reluctant modelling in the nude the young artist trades for access to Frenhofer's canvas. Once the exchange has been achieved, however, he and Pourbus find with dismay there is nothing to see "but a mass of confused color, crossed by a multitude of eccentric lines, making a sort of painted wall." Only one magically lifelike foot escapes from the morass. In Balzac's ultimate published version of the story (as reworked and expanded in 1837), Frenhofer awakens to the truth and kills himself after burning all of his work.[3]

Repeated and reconfigured many times by subsequent authors, Frenhofer's delusion has become an almost unendurable cliché.[4] But from another, more revealing angle, the character's melodramatic demise represents a colossal red herring. In the initial version of the story, Frenhofer never learns the truth and does not die. But Poussin's lover, Gillette, having been momentarily forgotten in the corner of the room, delivers the cold, concluding verdict to the ambitious young painter: "I believe that I already hate you."

The pathos of that ending thus lies not so much in Frenhofer's failure as it does in Gillette's agency having been bargained away for less than no return: "Nothing" is what Poussin and Pourbus perceive in Frenhofer's masterpiece. Beneath La Zambinella, Barthes declares, lies the "nothing of castration." Mme de Rochefide, whom the narrator in *Sarrasine* has been wooing with his narrative, echoes Gillette at its conclusion: "You have given me a disgust for life and for passions that will last a long time. . . . Leave me."[5] Both stories carry much the same lesson: excessive avidity for possession of the ideal comes to nullify social exchange and with it the possibility of signifying anything at all.

While Balzac was embellishing the Frenhofer story for its 1837 publication, he labored over another and more elaborate excursion into this body of myth, one that heightens the catastrophic melodrama of its predecessors while complicating the strict gender binarism that brings the other tales to their similar ends. *The Girl with the Golden Eyes* likewise narrates its protagonist's attempt to gain possession of a woman who represents a perfect exemplar of beauty never before possessed by any man.[6] Henri de Marsay, the bastard son of a philandering English lord, embodies the very image of the self-fashioned Parisian dandy. Along with an inherited fortune, impeccable dress, a darkly handsome exterior, and an effortlessly superior manner, Balzac steeps his protagonist in hyper-masculine prerogative via his membership in a preternaturally powerful secret society. The Zambinella of the tale is, at the outset, a young woman of unknown origin whom de Marsay (and *tout Paris*) first see in a carriage driven through the Tuileries Gardens. All who witness her passage are dumbstruck by her beauty, and de Marsay is consumed by it, vowing that the unapproachable beauty must be his and his alone.

Balzac pulls out all the stops in characterizing her overwhelming allure, rivalling "the most fervid, the most demonic inspiration of ancient genius: a sacred poem prostituted by those who have copied it for frescoes and mosaics, or by the bourgeois herd." What strikes him to the core, then, is in effect the ultimate original, "the very essence of woman, an abyss of pleasures whose depths may never be sounded," denatured by every interposition of imitative replicas, a being both prior to and beyond signification. So La Zambinella appeared to Sarrasine, and such cancellation of the many by the one spelt disaster both for him and for his doomed attempt to make art from that which obviates all imitation. In this successor tale, the unsurpassable ideal is no delusion; its consequences, all the more catastrophic.

When the eyes of the unknown paragon meet de Marsay's though her carriage window, their sexual pact is sealed, though a good deal of conventional cloak-and-dagger business intervenes. Her name, he discovers, is Paquita Valdes, and she lives sequestered in a fortress-like villa said to be owned by an aging Spanish grandee. She has made her startling public apparition owing only to the absence of her protector from the outwardly rundown pile to which de Marsay tracks the enigmatic beauty. At their assignation, however, de Marsay discovers a secret, soundproof retreat of luxuriant splendor, graced by a white cashmere divan fifty feet in circumference. During their first night of predictably rapturous union inside the isolated palace, Paquita insists de Marsay dress in women's clothes; on the second, she calls out in a moment of abandon, "Mariquita."

That name, he discovers, belongs to the actual lover and protector, who turns out to be another child of the far-ranging Lord
Dudley: his own Spanish half-sister and look-alike, Mariquita
Euphemia Porraberil, of whose existence he had been entirely unaware. The two siblings find themselves to have been loved as both
man and woman—or neither one. Each consumed by rage, jealousy,
and humiliation, the pair independently converge on Paquita's secret
chamber seeking murderous revenge. When de Marsay arrives, he
discovers his sister's having preceded him, the white divan soaked
in gore, and a terribly mutilated Paquita near death. In an instant,
brother and sister recognize one another and realize their shared
lover's essential innocence in loving them both. There the story
ends, the sister lamenting, "Nothing can console one for the loss of
what promised infinity."

Neither the zero of La Zambinella nor the infinity of Paquita Valdes
possesses value in any finite system of exchange. While no artist nor
work of art figures in *The Girl with the Golden Eyes*, Paquita suffers the
fate of Sarrasine's destroyed statue, just as de Marsay goes through
the same stages of heedless fascination, erroneous assumption, and
belated recognition as does the ill-fated sculptor. While Balzac was
compromising the poignant parsimony of his first *Unknown Masterpiece*, he was in this new novella breaking free from the gender binarism and economy of sexual exchange that had governed the two
earlier allegories. De Marsay finds himself to have been loved as a
woman; Mariquita retires to a convent in heartsick disillusionment
over her misdirected capacity for violence that surpassed that of
any male; Paquita's desire detaches itself from gender assignment
altogether. When her two lovers face one another over her corpse,
they appear as a sundered hermaphrodite, as the desire they had
shared suddenly short-circuits, diverted into mirrored mutual identity. Before irrevocably going their separate ways, brother and sister
embrace and kiss.

This excursion into Balzac beyond *Sarrasine* offers at least a partial remedy to the deficiency in Barthes's conclusion to *S/Z*. Might *Marat at His Last Breath* be seen to have provided a similar corrective? At the start, *S/Z* seemed a potentially useful instrument for a similarly extended unpacking of David's painting. At this point in the proceedings, however, it appears equally valid to view the *Marat* as an instrument for holding *S/Z* up to critical examination. Much as does the *Girl with the Golden Eyes*, the painting divides the female by incorporating its outwardly enticing imago into the male, who is unmanned by it, then leaving as a remainder the invisible but palpable virago steeped in blood. That female monster of revenge—implied by David's absent Corday, vividly characterized in Balzac's Mariquita—serves to absorb the opprobrium that would otherwise accrue to the male counterpart. While Balzac's fantasy glories in its violence, however, David's stilled monument sublimates it, that contrast in keeping with the greatly different briefs each work needed to satisfy, if not the contrasting capacities and limitations of their differing media. But gender positions in both escape strict biological assignment to migrate among the unstable collections of traits that constitute "character," whether on the page or on the canvas.

It is a pity, of course, that Balzac sets his web of non-binary exchanges amid a scenario awash in orientalist misogyny. The lovers' sequestered retreat bears all the hallmarks of a luxuriant hareem. To explain the savagery of Paquita's murder, Balzac descends further, attributing its appalling excesses to the female sex of its perpetrator, what he terms "that perfection of perfidy that distinguishes the weaker animals." Paquita's Circassian mother emerges to stand reproachfully over her daughter's corpse, only to be bought off with the bag of gold Mariquita flings at her feet, prompting a smile to cross the face of the venal crone. As it transpires, Paquita stands in for the perfected work of art not only on account of her flawless appearance, but because, having been sold originally to her lover by her mother, she became an item of property to be possessed or destroyed at will.

Balzac underlined these analogies to art by later adding a dedication to his contemporary Eugène Delacroix, the artist who most fashioned himself as the current leader and form-giver to the French school in the way that David had once been. In the intervening period, that role had been assumed by David's pupil Antoine-Jean Gros, who reinvented the grand historical canvas to serve Napoleon's need for spectacular reportage on his progress in arms across Europe. To this end, Gros markedly expanded the capacity of painting to encompass the patent facts of suffering and death, leaving behind the Academy's strictures, derived from Aristotle's *Poetics*, against overt depictions of violence as violations of tragic decorum. With Napoleon's fall and the restoration of the uninspiring Bourbon dynasty, Delacroix and like-minded heirs to the Revolution and the Empire sought examples of heroism further afield. Throughout the 1820s, the mind of that artist had thus been fixated on scenes of murder, destruction, and martyrdom set in the East.

•

Delacroix's monumental *Massacre at Chios*, exhibited in the Salon of 1824, bore witness (at a distance) to the slaughter in 1822 by Ottoman irregulars of some 25,000 inhabitants of that large and prosperous Greek island, with double that number dispatched to the slave markets. While there had been few roles for women on the battlefields painted by Gros, Delacroix rightly centered the pathos of his scene on the unimaginable suffering visited on the island's civilian population, who had been reluctantly embroiled in conflict (a refugee crisis of unprecedented proportions came in its wake).[7] The dispersed focus of Delacroix's composition accords with the undirected chaos of the event, acts of barbaric cruelty toward women and their unheard pleas dominating its foreground. Two semi-nude women frame the left side, one dead (whose child still seeks her breast), the other upright, manhandled onto the saddle of a mounted Turk, her arched, nude torso frontally displayed.

Two years later, the artist's *Greece Expiring on the Ruins of Missolonghi* [*page 130*] commemorated the atrocities in the disease-ridden, besieged city on the Gulf of Patras, whose desperate population largely perished in a poorly planned attempt to break free of the Turkish encirclement and bombardments they had endured for a year. That catastrophe occurred during the run of a benefit exhibition mounted in Paris on behalf of the Greek rebels. Before it had finished, Delacroix completed and hung his renowned allegory. Time and urgency recommended his economical condensation of the fragmented and multi-ethnic rebels into a singular, monumentalized female figure rising from the rubble, empty hands outstretched. Commonly characterized as helpless and vulnerable in a pathetic appeal for European rescue, this unmarked, upright updating of a classical Hera stands, however, unbowed over the male corpse immured in the fallen blocks of stone, as much a commanding woman, who will have her revenge, as she is the exemplary victim.

The stories of Ottoman slaughter and collective punishments circulated across Europe in graphic detail. Steeped in these word-pictures of the butchery visited on non-combatants, Delacroix then transposed their horror into literary fantasy with his *Death of Sardanapalus* of 1827–28. He borrowed its theme, but not its dénouement, from the 1821 play *Sardanapalus* by Lord Byron, who in 1824 had died in Missolonghi amid his exertions on behalf of the Greek cause. Even as the Greek revolt was nearing an almost miraculous success, Delacroix's memorial to the poet-hero lingers over the older imagery of defeat and carnage: the last Assyrian king, besieged by external enemies and internal insurrection, resolves to die rather than surrender. In the artist's words, from the catalogue of the exhibition, "Reclining on a superb bed at the summit of an immense pyre,

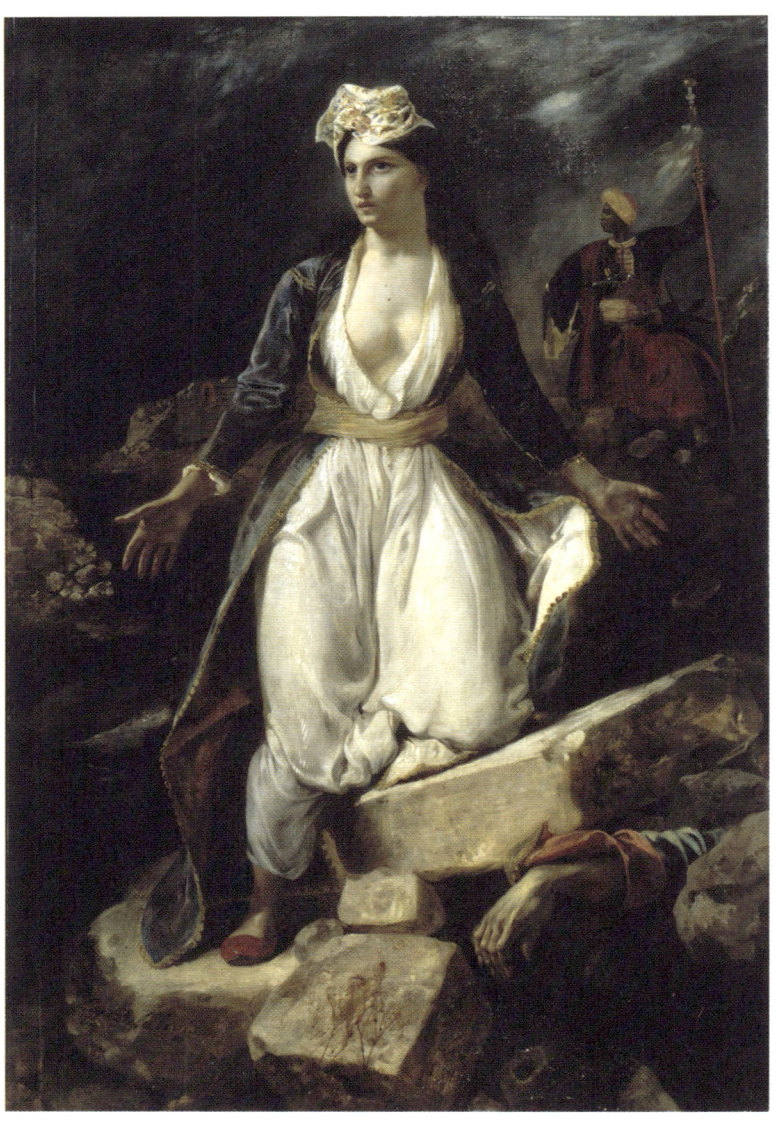

Eugène Delacroix, *Greece Expiring on the Ruins of Missolonghi*, 1826,
oil on canvas, 208 × 147 cm, Paris, Musée du Louvre

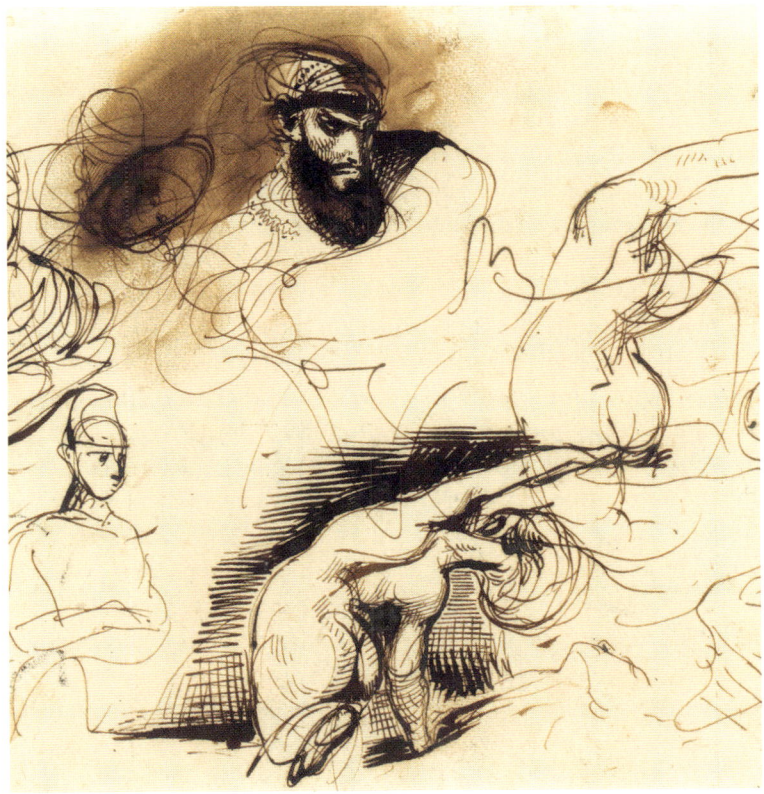

Eugène Delacroix, *The Death of Sardanapalus*, study, 1827, ink on paper,
Paris, Musée du Louvre (detail)

Sardanapalus gives the order to his eunuchs and the palace officers
to slaughter his women, his pages—even his horses and dogs so that
nothing that served his pleasure might survive him."[8]

An eloquent study for the painting, centered on the titular figure
and his main female victim, best conveys the intensity of its nihilistic
premise [*above*]. Balzac likens Henri de Marsay to similarly despotic

rulers, "the proudest of Caliphs, Pharaohs, or Xerxes, who believed themselves to be a race divine." But conjuring bloodshed and retribution would not, in the Paris of the mid-1830s, have depended upon distant atrocities or lurid tales of the exotic East. Stories of innocent victims of indiscriminate violence abounded at home, atrocities arising from unsuccessful republican uprisings in Paris and Lyon, many to be found in one soberly forensic treatise, *Memoir on the Events in the Rue Transnonain during the Days of 13 and 14 April 1834*, by the republican lawyer Alexandre Auguste Ledru-Rollin.[9] Its first paragraph contains this terse report: "In a single building in the rue Transnonain, twelve corpses lay horribly mutilated; four persons were grievously wounded: neither women, children, nor the aged were spared." There follows a literally blow-by-blow account of the murders by bullet and bayonet of these bystanders in the insurrection of those days, as government soldiers went door to door slaughtering and maiming in a frenzy of retribution, provoked by an erroneous report of sniper fire from an upper window. The fire brigade had broken down the stout main entrance, allowing the enraged troops to pour inside. Ledru-Rollin painstakingly gathered testimony from the surviving witnesses among the group of friends who had occupied the building, including a couple who operated a neighborhood theater on two upper floors. He juxtaposes the self-exculpating accounts of the soldiers against the physical evidence of bullet trajectories, deposits of blood, and inflicted injuries, reinforced by the vivid recollections of the residents.

Mme Poirier-Bonneville described the invading soldiers mounting to the second floor and pounding an unyielding door. An old man opened it, pleading, "We are peaceful people, unarmed, do not murder us." For his trouble, she relates, he was run through by three bayonets. As he lay moaning on the floor, the officer told him, "Old rogue, shut your trap or I'll do it for you." When a woman rushed from the adjacent room to help him, "a soldier turned on her and plunged his bayonet under her jaw and in this position fired a shot, the explosion scattering fragments of her head as far as the wall."[10] The incendiary accounts of heinous atrocities in the Greek War of Independence had come home, the same cruelties visited upon innocents caught in the way of insurgents vainly battling the authoritarian walls closing in, as the new monarchy of Louis-Philippe, installed in 1830, dropped all pretense of fulfilling the democratizing hopes aroused by that revolution.

Given how pervasive such graphic evocations of injury and death had become, passages like Balzac's description of Paquita's last moments do not stand out as extreme:

> The white room, where the blood showed so well, betrayed a long struggle. The prints of Paquita's hands were on the cushions. . . . Long strips of the tapestry had been torn down by her bleeding hands, which, without a doubt, had struggled long. . . . her bare feet had left their imprints on the edge of the divan, along which she must have run. Her body, mutilated by the dagger-thrusts of her executioner, told of the fury with which she had disputed a life that Henri had made precious to her.

The injuries left by the victim's teeth on her assailant's feet and breasts receive commensurate attention. Anything like this relish in forensic examination of Sarrasine's death at the hands of the cardinal's swordsmen would have shattered the mood and diction of that story, composed as it was in the last months before the revolutionary barricades made their reappearance. The cancellation of sexual exchange releases a quick, laconic spasm of violence in both *Sarrasine* and *The Unknown Masterpiece* (indeed barely perceptible in the latter). But the more charged and complicated choreography of desire in the *Girl with the Golden Eyes* yielded all the greater sum of destructive energy on its collapse. Well it might appear a poor bargain to transcend gender binaries in exchange for such luridly misogynistic violations of female bodies. But this new level of explicit mayhem could be traced to more than one source. The interval between 1830 and 1835 had seen a return of the sanguinary imagination of revolt, both in thought and deed, in line with the heyday of Marat more than four decades before. Historians' examinations of the cult of Marat have limited themselves to the months or the year or two following his assassination; but the spirit imputed to the martyr persisted for much longer, with a conspicuous resurgence precisely in this historical moment.

•

During the rapid unfolding of the 1830 Revolution, the elusiveness of credible authority permitted brief hopes that a new republic might emerge, dashed in part by the fecklessness of the marquis de Lafayette, one name surviving from the Great Revolution of 1789, his past betrayals of the patriot cause being conveniently overlooked. In the event, the duc d'Orléans, the heir to the dynastic line collateral to the Bourbons (descended from the brother of Louis XIV), became the default ruler, successfully installed by conservative forces intent on heading off anything approaching the egalitarianism of 1793. Consolidation of what was proudly called a "bourgeois" monarchy engendered a republican countermovement, partly overt and partly underground, that increasingly took its bearings from precisely that past era. As that dissenting movement evolved, its more moderate faction came to be called Girondins, their opponents naturally Montagnards, though the old lines could become confused. There had been the rehabilitation of Lafayette for a start, while the leader of the new Gironde, V.F. Raspail, was both a biographer and an unabashed admirer of Marat, the greatest enemy of both Lafayette and the former Gironde. The overarching republican organization even called itself the Société des Amis du Peuple. As censorship and repression tightened, however, the largely working-class Montagne tendency consolidated, organizing itself into "sections." Recalling the celebrated popular jurisdictions and assemblies of '93, they enjoyed no comparably official standing but did their best to stand in for them. As the historian Jill Harsin relates, "Each group of twenty chose a colorful and often provocative name: *Marat, Couthon, Saint-Just, Robespierre, Chute des Girondins* (Fall of the Girondins), *Quatre-vingt-treize* ('93), several *Montagnards* or *Montagnes, Jacobins, Guerre aux Châteaux* (War on the Palaces), *Paix aux Chaumières* (Peace to the Cottages), *Babeuf, Buonarroti, Incorruptible, Mort aux tyrans, 5 et 6 Juin, des Piques* (Pikes), *Tocsin, Barricade Méry, Insurrection de Lyon, 21 Janvier* (the date of the execution of Louis XVI), and *Louvel* (assassin of the duc de Berry)."[11]

While their members professed an educational mission, these nouveaux sections organized, as had their forebears, a network for strategizing and the stockpiling of weapons. They shared a common commitment to the second Declaration of Rights of Man and Citizen, the one promulgated by Robespierre in April 1793 as preamble to the new Jacobin constitution. Bloody but unsuccessful street insurrections eventuated from this cauldron in 1832 and 1834. As if that were not enough, the widowed, Bourbon duchesse de Berry returned from abroad to foment another Catholic uprising in the Vendée.

If there were to be a successor to *Marat at His Last Breath*, this ferment of revolutionary imagination and action would seem to be its most likely crucible. One could say that it demanded a *Marat* of its own. And it got one. The above recounting of the murderous havoc wreaked in the rue Transnonain would have sparked recognition in any follower of art, as that street name provides the title for Honoré Daumier's great lithograph of 1834 [*page 136*], in which he translated into unforgettable graphic form Ledru-Rollin's descriptions of the residents cut down in the dawn raid on that address.[12]

The relationship between David's martyr-prototype and the victims in Daumier's print can be gauged via the thoroughness with

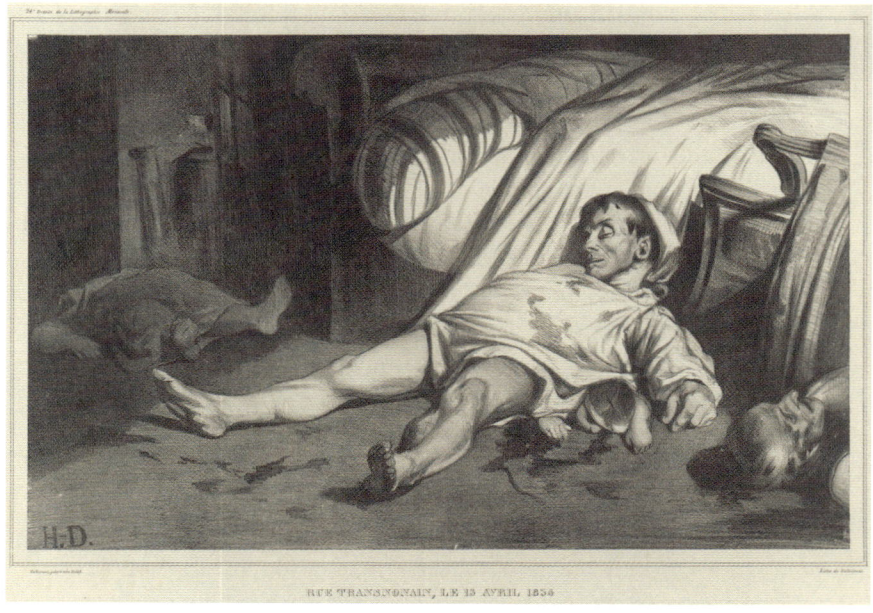

Honoré Daumier, *Rue Transnonain, le 13 avril 1834*, lithograph on paper, 28.6 × 44.1 cm

which the latter diametrically reverses nearly every defining characteristic of the *Marat*—such thoroughgoing reversals being, as noted
above, the far more motivated and decisive relationship than tepid
resemblance could ever be. In place of David's single, life-sized figure
emblazoned on an upright canvas, Daumier presents three genera-
tions of a family sprawled on the floor of their austere apartment.
While Marat hovers at the cusp between life and death, all present
in Daumier's martyr portrait have definitively left this life. David's
murdered subject had appeared in incomplete fragments, where
Daumier's fully illuminated male victim possesses the muscular
wholeness and integrity of a Renaissance dead Christ. The sexes,

fused by David, lie separately in the Daumier, the corpse of the man's wife lying supine in the shadows, their upturned feet composing a rhythmic counterpoint to the large shapes above. Where David had been sparing, Daumier's spilled blood is copious, the trail from the bayonet wound to the scalp of the small child joining the larger quantity emerging from under the nightshirt of its father, whose fallen mass presses the small body under its weight; the dark circle behind the head of the staring old man is not all shadow. David had lent the furnishings of Marat's equally austere chamber a stolid uprightness, while Daumier invests the overturned chair and bed linens with all the disruptive energy of the invasion that swept these lives away. And where the background to David's *Marat* is famously diffuse and insubstantial, Daumier's decisive handling of the lithographic crayon (composed from grease, wax, soap, soot, and shellac) yields a quasi-baroque massing and movement of forms like a roiling tempest, belying the modest size and insubstantial paper support that carries the drama. Daumier's *Rue Transnonain* could be said to de-sublimate the violence of Charlotte Corday's crime, the blood and tumult of her assault made endurable by his sublime graphic economy in a monochrome medium.

In his *Way of the Masks*, Claude Lévi-Strauss posits a rule of thumb bearing on the migration of signifying objects across transcultural boundaries: if the salient traits are preserved, their meaning will be reversed; conversely, if the meaning remains constant, the salient traits will be systematically reversed. For him, the boundaries in question were ethnic; in the case of David and Daumier, they were temporal, but there is a way, it strikes me, that Daumier's *Rue Transnonain* presents itself at the conclusion of this study with a kind of inevitability analogous to the way in which David's *Marat* had imposed itself on the start of my art-history career. The 1834 print differs from the 1793 painting as the revolutionary events of the July Monarchy differ from those of the First Republic. Daumier's comparatively fragile and ephemeral sheet arose from a time of bitterness and defeat. The future of the cause it espouses has been largely foreclosed, so it rests on the reproachful testimony of the immediate past, for which the vivid depiction of graphic violence provides essential witnessing. By so bearing witness, Daumier performs, albeit unwittingly, his most thoroughgoing reversal of David's prototype. The excluded details of Marat's murder and its aftermath find dramatic counterparts in Daumier's consummately executed crime scene. Only missing the bath, a sinewy, chemise-clad male victim sprawls in death; an over-turned chair echoes the one used by Laurent Bas to strike down and disarm Charlotte Corday; the victims have multiplied, but the general tumult and spilled blood approximate the confusion and disorder that confronted the local guard on the night of 13 July in the rue des Cordeliers. None of which would have been of use to David, as his contrasting expectation of success, of founding an entirely new and egalitarian social order, demanded concomitant permanence in its totemic image, one in no way exhausted by the immediate circum-stances of its making.

EPILOGUE

The indeterminate horizon of *Marat at His Last Breath* leaves its future relevance open to events and the evolution of democratic aspiration in directions that could never have been foreseen. And such has been its destiny, to which my opening account of discovery in postwar Los Angeles attests in its small way. Circumstances had then arisen such that David's martyr-portrait came into striking alignment with a waiting configuration of meanings. It only required playwright Peter Weiss to recognize and act on that convergence for the memory of this once-incendiary revolutionary to surface again. *The Persecution and Assassination of Jean-Paul Marat as Performed by the Inmates of the Asylum of Charenton under the Direction of the Marquis de Sade* resonated outward into the counterculture, not least via its central nervous system: popular music.

My introductory chapter called on the folk artist Judy Collins, who bannered the Brecht-and-Weill-inflected songs from the London production on her 1966 album *In My Life*. The following year, a distinctly different musical response to the play was released on *Forever Changes* [*page 140*], the song cycle by the African-American auteur Arthur Lee and his Los Angeles band Love—a landmark achievement fully on a par with better-known recorded monuments of the era like *Blonde on Blonde*, *Sgt. Pepper*, *Pet Sounds*, *Are You Experienced*, or *Eli and the Thirteenth Confession*.[1] Lee sings his most apocalyptic track,

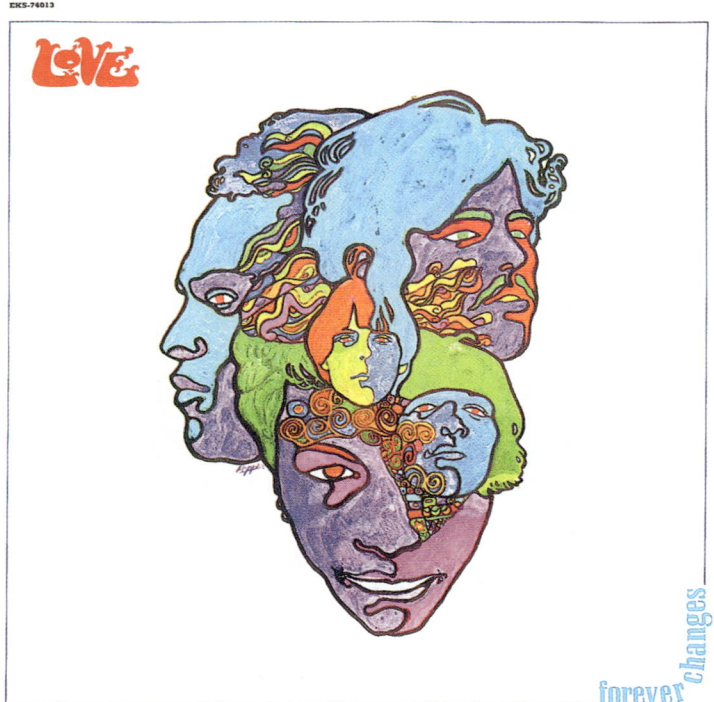

Love, *Forever Changes*, 1967, album cover, designer William S. Harvey, illustrator Bob Pepper, 30.48 × 30.48 cm

"The Red Telephone" (titled after the nuclear-emergency hotline between the Kremlin and the White House), in a paradoxically melli-fluous voice: "Sitting on a hillside, watching all the people die," he liltingly begins over strings and strummed acoustic guitar; its next line is one of suicidal resignation: "I'll feel much better on the other siide."

As the track nears its end, however, the tone changes, as Lee starts up a repeated chant:

> They're locking them up today
> They're throwing away the key
> I wonder who it will be tomorrow,
> You or me?

Then he abruptly breaks off to enunciate the line given by Weiss to the aroused patients in the asylum of Charenton:

> We're all normal, and we want our freedom!

Repetitions of the word "freedom" then pan in a sort of ghost voice across the stereo stage, before switching into caricatured "Black" diction, Lee descending an octave to intone the final words:

> All o' God's children gotta have their freedom.

The complexity of these juxtapositions calls for extended analysis, but let it be enough here to observe that the benediction of Marat floats above Lee's muted outcry over geo-political horrors, judicial persecutions, and thwarted Black aspirations. As much as Robert Wilson's rock-poster image of David's *Marat* had done, Lee's fragment from "Marat/Sade" reinforced my youthful fixation on the motif, which exercised a certain power to draw to itself otherwise vagrant impulses of discontent and contestation. I had fixed on a vocation as an art historian while resisting the available models (apart from my own teachers) for being one: a seeming dead end for an unknown student entering what proved to be a fiercely guarded domain.[2] I would not have been the first to adopt the painting as some kind of totemic shield—though never conceiving it in that way at the time.

My vocational decision came at a point when the violent atrocities unleashed on Indochina by Richard Nixon and Henry Kissinger re-ignited the outrage that had fueled the protests in Chicago during the Democratic Convention of 1968. The American invasion of Cambodia in April 1970 galvanized general campus populations to a degree not seen since the peak of the Mobilization two years before. The murder of four protesters at Kent State University in Ohio, inflicted by National Guardsmen in battle dress, brought home the distant violence of war in a way parallel to the savage repression of popular resistance in the Paris of 1834. It was also a moment when a major university president like Kingman Brewster of Yale would back his students and moneybag Republican trustees knew their place. Not only did Brewster offer his support for the strike over the Cambodian incursion, he had done likewise for the concurrent student demonstrations in support of the Black Panther Bobby Seale, who was facing trial in New Haven on trumped-up murder charges—the culmination of the sustained FBI campaign of persecution and assassination against the Panther leadership.

My previous book, *The Artist in the Counterculture*, published in 2023, narrated and examined these events. In hindsight, reliving that period may have helped bring my own long-buried Marat again to the forefront of my mind.[3] Before the full agonies of this epoch mounted, a totemic Marat had already been in place, bequeathed by the prescient Peter Weiss and invested with definitive form by the director Peter Brook. The playwright would have arrived at his core conception in advance of the earthshaking murder of the American President toward the end of 1963. But he would have had the examples before him of the 1961 assassinations in the newly liberated Congo of its first prime minister, Patrice Lumumba, and peacemaker Dag Hammarskjold, the Secretary-General of the United Nations. It was naturally disputed that the latter's plane had been shot down at the behest of Belgian mining interests, but valid suspicions would have been strongest in Stockholm, where Weiss was then living and working. Those deaths would be only the first in the reign of political murder that would stretch across the decade, lending the central motif of "Marat/Sade" its uncanny correspondence to events.

Weiss set his re-enactment of Marat's murder in 1808. At that date, the dominance of French armies in the theater of central Europe seemed secure. Despite terrifying losses during the previous year on the battlefield at Eylau (harrowingly memorialized on canvas by Gros), challenges from Prussia and Russia seemed to have been contained, and both were back in the fold of French alliances alongside a reduced Austria. It was not long before preparations were set in motion for Napoleon's marriage to the Habsburg princess Marie-Louise. But 1808 also saw the onset of popular rebellion against French usurpation of the Spanish throne. Francisco Goya's renowned print series, *The Disasters of War*, begun shortly afterward, memorializes an entirely different form of combat, one that gave the term *guerilla* to the world, an inconclusive, resource-draining insurgency against which conventional means of great-power warfare found poor purchase.

An historical witness of Weiss's acuity could not have failed to note the contemporary American parallels. The Charenton asylum director, guardian of social order, finds himself unprepared and overwhelmed at the play's conclusion by his own charges' intoning "We're all normal, and we want our freedom." Despite heightening the impairments of the inmates, Weiss takes them at their self-estimation: true madness inhabits the self-satisfied pillars of authority, who could not imagine how suddenly their security could collapse, just as the American establishment walked zombie-like toward disaster in thrall to the ever-receding chimera of victory in Vietnam. It was thus, as the decade played out, that the willfully deviant and deranged inhabitants of the counterculture came to claim the high ground of sanity, while the continual drumbeat of distant, criminally irrational violence sounded in the background.

Such were roughly the circumstances in which I was making up my mind to become, of all things, an historian of art—that is, to enter what was arguably then the most conservative and de-politicized of academic professions. But how to accomplish that without retreating from at least some moral alertness to the horrors in southeast Asia and consequent disaffection from anything tainted by conformity and conventional wisdom? I would not be the one to say I succeeded, but something new arose out of the attempt, a changed conception as to how eighteenth-century French art might be approached, one in which the Revolution and the struggle for emancipation from oppressive hierarchies would be central rather than belittled and marginalized as an unfortunate, anti-aesthetic interruption. Unnecessary warfare and acts of violence would be an inescapable part of that story, to be sure. Marat, who abhorred the former but promoted the latter, drew the salient strands of history into his thorny, contradictory person in such a way that the mission I set for myself as a naïve aspirant might well have waited for this book to reach its goal.

What might its notional predecessor have turned into, had I pur-sued it at the expense of the work that became *Painters and Public Life in Eighteenth-Century Paris*? An unanswerably counterfactual question to be sure. My visual *S/Z* would have relied far more on then-current theoretical abstractions and far less on any searching consideration of historical particularities. *Painters and Public Life* became my laboratory for winnowing the former and enhancing the latter. Not that the slings and arrows failed to arrive; among them, from a senior French scholar who effectively forbade its proposed translation, delaying by a decade the book's publication in France.[4] Perhaps a slighter Barthesean homage might have escaped hostile attention as something too eccentric to register—and thus no threat to any established interests. Who can say?

I do not now regret in the least that the sequence of work has unfolded as it has. Even had I realized that first impulse, I would now have wanted to revise and correct it into something like the present book. Better to do it only once, and that time in the 1980s was probably not its actual moment, which belonged in retrospect to the book I actually published. And I would cautiously suggest that there is something in the circumstances of early twenty-first-century history that might lend this present exercise a pertinence beyond the autobiography I have already spent too many words recounting.

In the main, *Murder in the Rue Marat* properly revolves around the dramatic events of 1793; its every observation and claim must be anchored there. But what carries over from the old graduate-student pipe dream is the heightened awareness that the latent meanings of those events remain salient into our present moment and whatever follows it. Beyond the enormity of America's 2024 election, I am thinking in part of contemporary art, both its practice and commentary, being as focused as it is on capturing equally contemporary currents of social emancipation and contestation. On the whole, this aspiration makes its case in the terms arising from urgent struggles against oppressive hierarchies across the board. All to the good. But need it ground itself so exclusively in the freshly deposited soil of the present?

Peter Brook's decisive and disruptive staging of "Marat/Sade" took place under the auspices of the Royal Shakespeare Company. Despite this hallowed name's standing in many quarters for revered high culture, that valence underwent its own transcoding in the crucible of the 1960s, Peter Brook serving once again as the conduit from theatrical experiments to the larger counterculture. In this instance, it was the dialogue on Shakespeare with his friend the Polish theater critic Jan Kott that drove his transformative productions from the Stratford repertory. Kott, born in 1914, had improbably survived the years of Nazi occupation as a left-wing, Jewish intellectual, then recouped by joining the postwar Communist regime as a cultural apparatchik. With the post-Stalinist thaw after 1956, he sought peers in the experimental milieu that included the visionary director Jerzy

Grotowski, instanced in the first chapter for his breaking down of the distinctions between spectator and performer. The latter spoke in the voice of nature, his prime exhibit being the bare life of the nomadic actor's body; but Kott chose the grandest inheritance of art.

Seeing Brook's touring production of *Titus Andronicus* in 1957 opened the critic's formerly Stalinist eyes to the power of an unflinching attitude toward the violence of this and many other plays in the Shakespeare canon—and thus their prefiguration of the atrocities of mid-twentieth-century Europe. In their ensuing friendship, Kott became as much the aesthetic instigator. His essay collection *Shakespeare Our Contemporary* appeared in English in 1964,[5] later to be joined on student bookshelves by Grotowski's equally influential *Towards a Poor Theatre* (both prefaced by Brook and both now largely forgotten).[6] Kott's title may suggest the Bard as cozy companion, but the contents of the book argued for anything but that. In his preface to the volume, Brook described him as "the only writer on Elizabethan matters who assumes without question that every one of his readers will at some point or other have been woken by police in the middle of the night."[7] That is the world of Arthur Lee's "Red Telephone," the reference being the surveillance and brutal ideological policing of the Soviet Bloc, aggravated during this era by restive, burgeoning movements for free expression from below.

Especially in Kott's kinetic paraphrasing of Shakespeare's Histories, it is their characters' ruthless indifference to life that Kott finds paramount, templates for grasping the bleak inhumanity of the power apparatus ("the Grand Mechanism" he calls it) that he had once served. As the political resistance mounted in America, any Black Panther or Chicago Seven defendant could testify to the reality earlier experienced by Kott's Polish readers. The mighty of the feudal order, as Kott articulated in his decisive analysis of *King Lear*, reduce themselves to the status of clowns and grotesques, in his time recapitulated by the bereft tramps of Samuel Beckett. Weiss's Charenton inmates, shuffling in their white, institutional garb, multiply the clown motif to proportions menacing to their keepers, embodying new power reassigned to the abject. In the province of the desiring body and mind, Kott's observations on the fluidity of the gender spectrum in the Sonnets and cross-dressing Comedies ran far ahead of the curve for its time, evincing an unembarrassed consideration of non-binary sexualities not to come into intellectual flower until well after the watershed Stonewall rebellion of 1969.

It is today rarely remembered that the 1960s were perhaps the last great era of common reading.[8] Such books were seized as handbooks and manuals for living an alternative life. Kott's transfigured the very heart of past literary art in doing so, and the closely contemporaneous revival of David's *Marat* by Peter Weiss worked to parallel effect. The time of Marat and David had likewise meant something to Parisian intellectuals when Fascism well and truly had them under its heel, just as it had to the beleaguered, defeated French republicans of 1834. If the resistant politics of those eras, with concomitant expressive aesthetics, nourished itself on the past—legacies that are the historian's province—then one wonders if the current practice of art history in the era of ICE and DOGE could make its deepest contribution less by donning the threads of the moment and more by bringing forward the charged repositories of experience that have sustained struggle before and could do so again.

ACKNOWLEDGMENTS

In keeping with this book's autobiographical turn, many people to whom I am gratefully indebted figure in the body of its text. But returning after a long interval to the French Revolution calls to mind invaluable colleagues whom I have not had the opportunity to thank in some years. French friends and colleagues, among them Régis Michel, Marie-Catherine Sahut, Philippe Bordes, Jean Clay, and the late Jacqueline Lichtenstein, offered welcome, wisdom, and encouragement to an unsure Californian as I made my way into the subject. In the UK, Alex Potts, the late David Bindman, Ting Chang, Sophie Matthiesson, and Mark Ledbury have all been valued companions along the way. I cannot imagine the long-ago inception of this project without Holly Clayson, Serge Guilbaut, and Mimi Yiepruksawan. Alex, Mark, and Serge offered insightful readings of its long-postponed outcome, as did Andrei Pop, Ewa Lajer-Burcharth, Richard Meyer, Rob Slifkin, Jonathan Weinberg, and Lauren Rooney. Daniella Berman's deep research into the unfinished art of the Revolution helped bring the entire period back into focus. And the deft image manipulations by Dominika Ivanická fulfilled my long-standing dream of interpretation proceeding in the visual domain. I profoundly thank them all. Nor would I have come to the point of embarking on the project in earnest without having discussed the problems of David's *Marat* over several years in my foundation-course presentations to the first-year students at the Institute of Fine Arts.

Gillian Malpass was my first editor and book designer, and there has never been anyone else to match her combined sympathy and acuity, which she brought to the present volume as fully as ever. My publisher, Michelle Komie, graciously and enthusiastically welcomed another book of mine to Princeton University Press, while the publications coordinator, Annie Miller, managing editor, Terri O'Prey, and production manager, Steven Sears, ably held the strands of production in their hands. Emma Brown performed the invaluable work of obtaining images and permissions. I am likewise in debt to the redoubtable Xin Wang and to the artist for the reproduction of Yue Minjun's *Death of Marat*.

As ever and as always, my reliance on the loving support and unerring good judgment of Catherine Phillips remains beyond measure.

NOTES

I SCENE-SETTING PROLOGUE

1 Michael Coveney, "Marat/Sade: The Play that Began a Stage Revolution," *Guardian* (4 October 2011), https://www.independent.co.uk/arts-entertainment/theatre-dance/features/marat-sade-the-play-that-began-a-stage-revolution-2365086.html#.

2 Otto-Karl Werckmeister, "A Critique of T. J. Clark's *Farewell to an Idea*," *Critical Inquiry* (XXVIII: 4, 2002), 861. Clark's extended discussion of David's *Death of Marat* can be found in *Farewell to an Idea: Episodes from a History of Modernism* (New Haven and London: Yale University Press, 1999), 15–53; see note 12 below.

3 See Rebecca McGrew and Glenn Phillips, eds., *It Happened at Pomona: Art at the Edge of Los Angeles* (Claremont, Calif.: Pomona College Museum of Art, 2011); also, Thomas Crow, *The Artist in the Counterculture:From Bruce Conner to Mike Kelley and Other Tales from the Edge* (Princeton, N.J.: Princeton University Press, 2023), 149–71.

4 Vincent Descombes, *Modern French Philosophy* (originally *Le Même et l'autre*), trans. L. Scott-Fox and J. M. Harding (Cambridge and New York: Cambridge University Press, 1980), 105.

5 Claude Lévi-Strauss, *The Savage Mind* (Chicago and London: University of Chicago Press, 1966), 23; Roberto Calasso, *The Marriage of Cadmus and Harmony*, trans. Tim Parks (New York: Vintage, 1993), offers the most intricately nuanced synthesis of the Greek mythological corpus, but, nonetheless, echoes Lévi-Strauss in asserting, "There is no such thing as an isolated mythical event, just as there is no such thing as an isolated word. Myth, like language, gives all of itself in each of its fragments. When a myth brings into play repetition and variants, the skeleton of the system emerges for a while, the latent order, covered in seaweed."

6 Roland Barthes, *S/Z: Essais* (Paris: Editions du Seuil, 1970); for an edited edition of the seminar's proceedings, see Claude Coste and Andy Stafford, eds., *Roland*

Barthes: Sarrasine de Balzac. Séminaires à l'Ecole pratiques des hautes études 1967–1968, 1968–1969 (Paris: Editions du Seuil, 2011).

7   The seemingly feminine ending of the protagonist's name leads Barthes (lexie x) to twin it with the French proper name Sarrazin, with its clearly masculine ending. Joining the contrasting sibilants by a slash parallels the downstroke of the Z and graphically evokes the theme of a cut.

8   See Honoré de Balzac, *Correspondance*, 1: *1809–1833*, ed. R. Pierrot (Paris, 1960), 39, 46.

9   Honoré de Balzac, "Sarrasine," in Barthes, *S/Z*, 256; see translation by Richard Miller, *S/Z* (New York: Hill and Wang, 1974), 253.

10   See Thomas Crow, *Emulation: David, Drouais, and Girodet in the Art of Revolutionary France*, 2nd ed. (New Haven and London: Yale University Press, 2006), 117–44.

11   Arnold Rubin, "Accumulation: Power and Display in African Sculpture," *Artforum* (May 1975), 35–47; see "Influences: Betye Saar," *Frieze* (October 2016), https://www.frieze.com/article/influences-betye-saar#:~:text=The%20Watts%20Towers%20were%20a,how%2cto%20be%20an%20artist A partial record of Rubin's research and pedagogy can be found in Rubin, *Art as Technology: The Arts of Africa, Oceania, Native America, and Southern California*, ed. Zena Pearlstone (Catskill, N.Y.: Hillcrest Press, 1989). Rubin's premature death in 1988 deprived the field of a fuller realization of his multi-faceted contributions and intellect.

12   Klaus Herding speaks in an apposite way in his essay on the multi-temporal character of the painting ("La Notion de temporalité chez David à partir du Marat," in Régis Michel ed., *David contre David* [Paris: La Documentation Française, 1993], 1: 424: "Plus on pénètre dans les multiples paradoxes que contient ce tableau, plus on y trouvera des éclairissements quand on y applique, en la modifiant, une terminologie qui nous suggère de recevoir un tableau non comme un bloc, mais comme un complexe d'idées qui vise, telle une tête de Janus, le passé et le future." A contrary thesis has been offered by T. J. Clark, who, as noted above, was my graduate advisor when I left behind my early ambition to fashion a visual *S/Z* from David's *Marat*. When he later decided to write on the painting himself ("Painting in Year II," see note 2 above), he did so by advancing the hypothesis that David's conception was distinguished by possessing "no usable pasts," thus marking a decisive historical rupture and point of origin for artistic "modernism" in the nineteenth and twentieth centuries. Such a thesis may be understandable from a scholar whose main concerns lie in the second half of the nineteenth century or later; but there is no real bridge between that supposition and the concerns of the present study, in which a good number of "usable pasts" lie at the heart of the interpretation.

2 DIVISION

1 I first pointed out the correspondence in *Emulation: Making Artists for Revolutionary France* (New Haven and London: Yale University Press, 1995, 166–69), but there made limited use of the recognition.

2 Anne-Louis Girodet, Letter to Benoît-François Trioson (19 Jan. 1793), in Girodet, *Œuvres posthumes,* ed. P.A. Coupin (Paris, 1829), II, 424–25.

3 For documents, see Crow, *Emulation: David, Drouais, and Girodet in the Art of Revolutionary France,* 2nd ed. (New Haven and London: Yale University Press, 2006), 150.

4 Michel Dorat-Cubières, *La Mort de Basseville ou la conjuration de Pie VI dévoilée* (Paris, 1793).

3 FUSION

1 Rebecca Comay, "Tabula Rasa: David's 'Death of Marat' and the Trauma of Modernity," in Marius Mjaaland and Ulrik Rasmussen, eds., *Impossible Time: Past and Future in the Philosophy of Religion* (Tübingen: Mohr Siebeck Verlag, 2012), 140.

2 See Ian Germani, *Jean-Paul Marat: Hero and Anti-Hero of the French Revolution* (Queenston, Ontario: Edwin Mellen Press, 1992), 59–60; Jacques Ghilhaumou, *La Mort de Marat* (Paris: Editions Complexe, 1989), 85–86.

3 Jacques Ghilhaumou, "La Mort de Marat à Paris (13–17 juillet 1793)," in Jean-Claude Bonnet, ed., *La Mort de Marat* (Paris: Flammarion, 1986), 63.

4 Guillaumou, *La Mort de Marat,* 56, 64–67.

5 See ibid., 37–40.

6 See Olivier Coquard, *Jean-Paul Marat* (Paris: Fayard, 1993), 368.

7 See Gilhaumou, *La Mort de Marat,* 72–73.

8 Ibid., 74–75.

9 Helen Weston, "The Corday-Affair: No Place for a Woman," in Weston and William Vaughan, eds., *The Death of Marat* (Cambridge and New York: Cambridge University Press, 200), 144.

10 Jean-Rémy Mantion, "Enveloppes à Marat David," in Bonnet, *La Mort de Marat,* 218.

11 See Coquard, *Marat,* 370, 412.

12 See the indispensable Morris Slavin, *The Making of an Insurrection: Parisian Sections and the Gironde* (Cambridge, Mass., and London: Harvard University Press, 1986), 21.

13 Ibid., 112.

14   A landmark study of David's *Marat* on this theme is Klaus Herding, "Davids Marat als dernier appel à l'unité révolutionnaire," *Idea: Jahrbuch der Hamburger Kunsthalle,* 2 (1983), 89–112.

15   See Morris Slavin, "Jacques Roux: A Victim of Vilification," *French Historical Studies* (Autumn 1964), 529–32.

16   Ibid., 533.

17   See Paul R. Hanson, *The Jacobin Republic under Fire: The Federalist Revolt in the French Revolution* (University Park, Pa.: Pennsylvania State University Press, 2003), 25–26.

18   See Germani, *Jean-Paul Marat*, 53.

19   See David L. Dowd, "Jacques-Louis David, Artist Member of the Committee on General Security," *American Historical Review* (July 1952), 873–79.

20   See M. de Barghon-Fortrion, ed., *Mémoire écrit par Marie-Thérèse-Charlotte de France sur la captivité des princes et princesses, ses parents, depuis le 10 Août 1792* (Paris: 1858), 74; affirmed by Charles-Eloi Vial, *Marie-Antoinette* (Paris: Perrin, 2023), 561.

21   See Xavier Salmon, in Salmon and Pierre Arizzoli-Clémentel, eds., *Marie-Antoinette*, exh. cat. (Paris: Galeries nationales du Grand Palais, 2008), 35; Salmon expresses mild reservations but does not alter the traditional attribution in his catalogue entry.

22   See Will Bashor, *Marie Antoinette's Darkest Days : Prisoner No. 280 in the Conciergerie* (Lanham, MD: Rowman and Littlefield, 2016), 237–47.

23   See the invaluable study by Guillaume Mazeau, *Le Bain de l'histoire: Charlotte Corday et l'attentat contre Marat (1793–2009)* (Paris: Champ Vallon, 2009), 181.

4   CIRCULATION

1   The reports are reproduced in Guillaume Mazeau, *Le Bain de l'histoire: Charlotte Corday et l'attentat contre Marat (1793–2009)* (Paris: Champ Vallon, 2009), 355.

2   Ibid., 69–7.

3   Her speech is reproduced in ibid., 385: "je veux que mon dernier soupir soit utile à mes concitoyens, que ma tête portée dans Paris soit un signe de ralliement pour tous les amis des lois, que la montagne chancelante voit sa perte écrite avec mon sang, que je sois leur dernière victime et que l'univers vengé déclare que j'ai bien mérité de l'humanité."

4   Bibliothèque nationale de France, Recueil. Collection de Vinck. Un siècle d'histoire de France par l'estampe, 1770–1870, vol. XXXII (pièces 5252–5394), Ancien Régime et Révolution, https://catalogue.bnf.fr/ark:/12148/cb40261215w. Genetic analysis of

the blood traces for both human and non-human DNA yielded new precision concerning the possible microbial cause of his painful skin condition, but no resolution,
as it suggests more than one pathogen at work. See Toni De Dios et al., "Metage-
nomic Analysis of a Blood Stain from the French Revolutionary Jean-Paul Marat
(1743-1793)," *Infection, Genetics and Evolution*, doi: 10.1016/j.meegid.2020.104209,
https://www.biorxiv.org/content/10.1101/825034v2; for a journalistic summary, see
Marc Gozlan, "Des Biologistes moléculaires font parler le sang du révolutionnaire
Marat," *Le Monde* (11 Nov. 2019), https://www.lemonde.fr/blog/realitesbiomedicales/
2019/11/08/des-biologistes-moleculaires-font-parler-le-sang-du-revolutionnaire-
marat/

5   See Peter McPhee, *Robespierre: A Revolutionary Life* (New Haven and London:
Yale University Press, 2012), 124.

6   See Morris Slavin, *The Making of an Insurrection: Parisian Sections and the
Gironde* (Cambridge, Mass., and London: Harvard University Press, 1986), 64-75.

7   Quoted in Clifford D. Conner, *Jean Paul Marat: Scientist and Revolutionary*
(New York: Humanity Books, 1997), 108.

8   See McPhee, *Robespierre*, 131; for a concise account of David's involvements in
subsequent parliamentary and Jacobin affairs, see Philippe Bordes, "'Brissotin enragé,
ennemi de Robespierre': David, conventionnel et terroriste," in Régis Michel ed., *David
contre David* (Paris: La Documentation Française, 1993), I: 319-45.

9   For a discussion, see Philippe Roger, "L'Homme de sang: l'invention sémio-
tique de Marat," in Jean-Claude Bonnet, ed., *La Mort de Marat* (Paris: Flammarion,
1986), 141-65.

10   See Olivier Coquard, *Jean-Paul Marat* (Paris: Fayard, 1993), 373.

11   See ibid., 373-75.

12   Guillaume Mazeau, *Le Bain de l'histoire: Charlotte Corday et l'attentat contre
Marat (1793-2009)* (Paris: Champ Vallon, 2009), 142-46.

13   For an inventory of the David's departures from the actual details of the murder
scene, see Jörg Traeger, "La Mort de Marat et la religion civile," in Michel, *David contre
David*, I: 403.

14   Mazeau, *Le Bain de l'histoire*, 148

5   DEFINITION

1   Roland Barthes, *S/Z: Essais* (Paris: Editions du Seuil, 1970), lexie LIX.

2   Ibid., lexie LIIIVII.

3   Rebecca Comay, "Tabula Rasa: David's 'Death of Marat' and the Trauma of

Modernity," in Marius Mjaaland and Ulrik Rasmussen, eds., *Impossible Time: Past and Future in the Philosophy of Religion* (Tübingen: Mohr Siebeck Verlag, 2012), 142.

4   For a convincing approximation of what a more conventional perspective might look like, see the front cover of the 2019 LP by Andrew Bird, "My Finest Work Yet," for which David's setting was meticulously reconstructed as a three-dimensional set, credited to the designer Sage LaMonica and the photographer Amanda Demme, into which Bird inserts himself costumed as the expiring Marat.

5   See Ian Germani, *Jean-Paul Marat: Hero and Anti-Hero of the French Revolution* (Queenston, Ontario: Edwin Mellen Press, 1992), 73.

6   See, for a representative formulation, Jean-Paul Sartre, *Being and Nothingness: An Essay in Phenomenological Ontology*, trans. Sarah Richmond (New York: Washington Square Press, 2018), 9–10.

7   Jean-Paul Sartre, *Nausea*, trans. Richard Howard (New York: New Directions, 2013), 122, 126.

6   BEYOND DEFINITION

1   Jean-Paul Sartre, *Being and Nothingness: An Essay in Phenomenological Ontology*, trans. Sarah Richmond (New York: Washington Square Press, 2018), 57.

2   Ibid., 25.

3   See C. Defeyt, D. Marechal, F. Vandepitte, et al., "Rethinking Jacques-Louis David's *Marat assassiné* through Material Evidences," *Heritage Science* (2023), https://doi.org/10.1186/s40494-023-00861-3.

4   Sartre, *Being and Nothingness*, 800.

5   On Paulze in particular, see Mary Vidal, "David among the Moderns: Art, Science, and the Lavoisiers," *Journal of the History of Ideas* (Oct. 1995), 611–23.

6   G. W. F. Hegel, *Hegel's Phenomenology of Spirit*, trans. A. V. Miller (Oxford University Press, 1977), 17 and throughout. The distinction is fundamental to Hegel's parable of the primordial victory, in their struggle for recognition, of the master over the slave, whereby the victorious master attains recognized selfhood, that is, being-for-itself, but at the expense of participating in active, transformative engagement with the stuff of the world (104–19). With the master perpetually idle and only a consumer, that labor falls to the slave, first in abject, thing-like servitude, but over time becoming the route to a superior, more complete being-for-itself as fully enmeshed in historical change. In the Hegel interpretation most adjacent to Sartre, that of Alexandre Kojève, *Introduction to the Reading of Hegel*: Lectures on the *Phenomenology of Spirit*, ed. Raymond Queneau and Alan Bloom, trans. James Nichols (Ithaca, N.Y.:

Cornell University Press, 1969), a close reading on this topic (3–30) serves "In Place of an Introduction." On the central importance of Kojève's interwar lectures on Hegel to the conduct of philosophy in Paris, see Vincent Descombes, *Modern French Philosophy* (originally *Le Même et l'autre*), trans. L. Scott-Fox and J. M. Harding (Cambridge and New York: Cambridge University Press, 1980), 27–48.

7   Maurice Merleau-Ponty, *Humanism and Terror: An Essay on the Communist Problem*, trans. John O'Neill (Boston: Beacon Press, 1990), 36–37. The italics are in the original.

8   Proceedings of Convention Nationale (25 Frimaire year II [15 Dec. 1793]), *Moniteur universel* (27 Frimaire year II [17 Dec. 1793]), in *Réimpression de l'Ancien Moniteur. . . . Mai 1789–Nov. 1799* (Paris 1847), XVIII, 678.

9   See proceedings of Convention Nationale (10 Prairial year II [29 May 1794]), *Moniteur universel* (12 Prairial year II [31 May 1794]), in *Réimpression de l'Ancien Moniteur*, XX, 603–604.

10   Proceedings of Convention Nationale (8 Nivôse year II [28 Dec. 1793]), *Moniteur universel* (10 Nivôse year II [30 Dec. 1793]), in *Réimpression de l'Ancien Moniteur*, XIX, 82.

11   Rebecca Comay, "Tabula Rasa: David's 'Death of Marat' and the Trauma of Modernity," in Marius Mjaaland and Ulrik Rasmussen, eds., *Impossible Time: Past and Future in the Philosophy of Religion* (Tübingen: Mohr Siebeck Verlag, 2012), 142, sees in the "insistent accumulation of brushstrokes and anxiously pulsating paint" of the *Bara* "a clash between the redemptive standstill of the revolutionary now-time and the unfinished order of history, between singularity and repetition, between standstill and flux."

12   Translations from Charles Martin, trans., *Ovid: Metamorphoses* (New York: Norton, 2004).

13   Roland Barthes, *A Lover's Discourse, Fragments*, trans. Richard Howard (New York: Hill and Wang, 1978), 15.

14   Interview published in *Les Lettres françaises* (20 May 1970); quoted in Claude Coste and Andy Stafford, eds., *Roland Barthes: Sarrasine de Balzac*, 29.

15   Avant-propos, in Coste and Stafford, *Roland Barthes*, 42.

16   As the critic Barbara Johnson put it as early as 1978 ("The Critical Difference," *Diacritics* [Summer 1978], 6), "If Barthes is really attempting to demystify the ideology of totality, and if his critical strategy implicitly gives a positive value to castration, why does his analysis of Balzac's text still seem to take castration at face value as an unmitigated and catastrophic horror?"

17   See Chapter 1, p. 14 and n. 4.

7   THE NEW *MARAT*

1   Translations from Charles Martin, trans., *Ovid: Metamorphoses* (New York: Norton, 2004).

2   Honoré de Balzac, "Le Chef d'oeuvre inconnu," in Pierre-Georges Castex, ed., *La Comédie humaine* (Paris: Gallimard, Bibliothèque de la Pléiade, 1979), x, 413–38.

3   See Pierre Laubriet, *Un Catéchisme esthétique: Le Chef-d'œuvre inconnu de Balzac* (Paris; Didier, 1961), 11–16, for the early publishing history of the story; the 1831 and 1837 endings are reproduced side by side on p. 238.

4   See Paul Barolsky, "The Fable of Failure in Modern Art," *VQR* (Summer 1997), https://www.vqronline.org/essay/fable-failure-modern-art.

5   "Sarrasine," in Roland Barthes, *S/Z: Essais* (Paris: Editions du Seuil, 1970), 253.

6   Honoré de Balzac, "La Fille aux yeux d'or," in Rose Fortassier, ed., *La Comédie humaine* (Paris: Gallimard: Bibliothèque de la Pléiade, 1977), V, 1528–68.

7   See Mark Mazower, *The Greek Revolution: 1821 and the Making of Modern Europe* (New York and London: Penguin, 2021), 149–52.

8   Livret, Salon de 1827 (Paris, 1828); see Lee Johnson, *The Paintings of Eugène Delacroix: A Critical Catalogue* (Oxford: Oxford University Press, 1981), 1: 114–15.

9   Alexandre Auguste Ledru-Rollin, *Memoir on the Events in the Rue Transnonain during the Days of 13 and 14 April 1834*, https://gallica.bnf.fr/ark:/12148/bpt6k5668134q.textelmage.

10   Ibid., 17–18.

11   Jill Harsin, *Barricades: The War of the Streets in Revolutionary Paris, 1830–1848* (New York and Basingstoke: Palgrave, 2002), 66.

12   Literature on the print is surprisingly sparse, but see the brief discussion in Mechtild Widrich, *Monumental Cares: Sites of History and Contemporary Art* (Manchester: Manchester University Press, 2023), 179–89.

EPILOGUE

1   The artists being, respectively, Bob Dylan, the Beatles, the Beach Boys, the Jimi Hendrix Experience, and Laura Nyro. Love's lead guitarist, Johnny Echols, relates his seeing the *Marat/Sade* film with Lee and the writing of "The Red Telephone": "It was about those people in the nuthouse. I remember right after we saw that, Arthur started humming those words here and there." See Andrew Sandoval, notes in the booklet accompanying the augmented CD reissue of *Forever Changes* (Elektra and Rhino Records, 2008).

2   On some of the reasons for this condition, see Thomas Crow, "The Practice of Art History in America," *Daedalus* (Spring 2006), 74–80.

3   See Thomas Crow, *The Artist in the Counterculture: From Bruce Conner to Mike Kelley and Other Tales from the Edge* (Princeton, N.J.: Princeton University Press, 2023), 125–29.

4   Thomas Crow, *La Peinture et Son Public à Paris au XVIIIe Siècle* (Paris: Editions Macula, 2000).

5   Jan Kott, *Shakespeare Our Contemporary*, trans. Borislaw Taborski (New York and London: Norton, 1964).

6   Jerzy Grotowski, *Towards a Poor Theatre* (London: Methuen, 1968).

7   Peter Brook, preface to Kott, *Shakespeare Our Contemporary*, n.p.

8   For a useful guide, see Philip D. Beidler, *Scriptures for a Generation: What We Were Reading in the '60s* (Athens, Ga.:University of Georgia Press, 1995).

INDEX

PHOTOGRAPH CREDITS

© De Vinck collection, Cabinet des estampes, Bibliothèque nationale, Paris: p. 68

© Granamour Weems Collection / Alamy Stock Photo: p. 140

Photo © Photo Josse / Bridgeman Images: p. 71

© LACMA, The Ciechanowiecki Collection, Gift of The Ahmanson Foundation: p. 71

© Heritage Image Partnership Ltd. / Alamy Stock Photo: p. 47

© Marat Sade Productions—Royal Shakespeare Company, Alamy Stock Photo: p. 5

© 1966, Metro-Goldwyn-Mayer Studios Inc. All Rights Reserved. Courtesy of MGM Media Licensing: p. 7

© Metropolitan Museum of Art, The Jules Bache Collection, 1949: p. 101

© Metropolitan Museum of Art, Purchase, Mr. and Mrs. Charles Wrightsman Gift, in honor of Everett Fahy, 1977: p. 103

© Metropolitan Museum of Art, Rogers Fund, 1920: pp. 118, 136

© MIT Libraries: pp. 30, 38

© Peter Barritt / Alamy Stock Photo: p. 113

© RMN-Grand Palais / Art Resource, NY: pp. 18, 33, 42, 43, 52, 61, 84, 111, 120, 121, 130, 131

© Royal Museums of Fine Arts of Belgium, Brussels / J. Geleyns - Art Photography: pp. ii, vi, 26, 30, 38, 40, 53, 63, 82, 87, 92

© SIPA Press/SIPA USA: p. 11

© Courtesy of Yue Minjun Studio: p. 20

Copyright © 2025 by Thomas Crow

Princeton University Press is committed to the protection of copyright and the intellectual property our authors entrust to us. Copyright promotes the progress and integrity of knowledge created by humans. By engaging with an authorized copy of this work, you are supporting creators and the global exchange of ideas. As this work is protected by copyright, any reproduction or distribution of it in any form for any purpose requires permission; permission requests should be sent to permissions@press.princeton.edu. Ingestion of any PUP IP for any AI purposes is strictly prohibited.

Published by Princeton University Press, 41 William Street, Princeton, New Jersey 08540
In the United Kingdom: Princeton University Press, 99 Banbury Road, Oxford OX2 6JX
press.princeton.edu

GPSR Authorized Representative: Easy Access System Europe
Mustamäe tee 50, 10621 Tallinn, Estonia, gpsr.requests@easproject.com

All Rights Reserved
ISBN 978-0-691-27444-7
ISBN (ebook) 978-0-691-27443-0
Library of Congress Control Number: 2025932476
British Library Cataloging-in-Publication Data is available

Editorial: Michelle Komie and Annie Miller
Production Editorial: Terri O'Prey
Text and Jacket Design: Gillian Malpass
Production: Steven Sears
Publicity: Jodi Price
Printed in China
10 9 8 7 6 5 4 3 2 1

JACKET IMAGE: Yue Minjun, *The Death of Marat* (detail), 2002, oil on canvas, 290 × 219 cm. Private collection. Courtesy of Yue Minjun Studio
FRONTISPIECE Jacques-Louis David, *Marat at His Last Breath* (detail), 1793, oil on canvas, 165 × 182 cm., Brussels, Musées royaux d'Art et d'Histoire

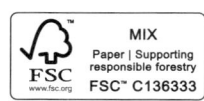